Get Found Now!

Search Engine Optimization
Secrets Exposed

Learn How to Achieve High Search Rankings in Google, Yahoo and Bing

By

Richard Geasey
and
Shannon Evans

Practical Local Search

Local Search Marketing and SEO Consulting

Bellevue and Seattle WA

www.practicallocalsearch.com

ISBN
1449986390
9781449986391

First Edition
January 2010

Cover Design:
Carrie Tatum
Bainbridge Island, WA

with a little help from

Matthew Mikulsky of Chatter Creative
Richard Geasey
Shannon Evans

Practical Local Search

Local Search Marketing and SEO Consulting

Bellevue and Seattle WA

www.practicallocalsearch.com

Dedication

Since Richard and I met a little over a year ago in December 2008 we have met and talked with hundreds if not thousands of small business owners. Every one of them expressed the same questions and concerns regardless of their profession and their target audience: How do we get people to come to our website and then to convert that visit into an action?

So we set out to find what sort of advice was out there for the small business owner that they could rapidly implement. We started looking on the Internet and found a little here, a little there, but not much was useful for a person with a non-technical background. Then we trekked to the Seattle library smack in the middle of the cyber universe in search of books and magazines that might have resources we could recommend to our colleagues. Again, not much was found and certainly nothing in clear straightforward language easy to implement by an individual or small business owner. Notta. Zero. Zilch.

We began to create content that we could then take back to our clients and fellow business owners and deliver in a workshop forum. This resulted in action guides and teaching notes and hundreds of PowerPoint slides and excess information we thought was nice but could never find the time to squeeze in a standing room only workshop. We began crafting the first book from our workshop series Get Found Now, Local Search Secrets Exposed (now on Amazon and doing well). So we began work on the next book Get Found Now! Twitter Techniques and Strategies for the Small Business Owner. In the editing process we found a huge gap in the discussion of Search Engine Optimization targeted for the small business owner's website.

Out came the teaching notes, blog entries, action guides, and PowerPoint slides and we knew we had to get a book on SEO out to our readers ASAP. The economy was in the crapper and our friends were withering on the vine with websites that were not working for them. Get Found Now! Search Engine Optimization Secrets Exposed was born.

Get Found Now! SEO Secrets Exposed is designed specifically for small business owners who have busy lives and limited marketing resources. While a pretty website with all the bells and whistles is great to have, it does a business no good if it can't be found by potential customers and clients. SEO is one of the cornerstones for getting a website configured in such a way that it gets exposure to the right audience on the web. This book takes a look at SEO from the traditional perspective of website and blog design and then takes it a step further to look at how to optimize the more popular social media sites for even more web traffic.

We hope that this book is easy to use and results in improved traffic and search engine rankings for your website, blog, and social media pages. If you get great results after following our suggestions, please send us an update. We would love to hear from you. If you get rich off of our ideas, please buy multiple copies of our books and share them with your friends. Royalties are important to poor authors like Rich and me!

Good luck and get going!

Shannon Evans
Richard Geasey

The man at the top of the mountain did not fall there.

Anonymous

Practical Local Search

Local Search Marketing and SEO Consulting

Bellevue and Seattle WA

www.practicallocalsearch.com

Preface

This book is about search engine optimization for the novice. It is less a "how to" than a "why you should" book. To most people the phrase "search engine optimization" conjures up visions of a sorcerer playing around with your web site. The fact is in many instances the changes are easy and quick to make. Best of all, the benefits to you and the business your web site represents are substantial.

You will find throughout this document a pronounced bias towards Google. I live but a short drive from the Microsoft campus and despite their army of extremely talented professionals they still can't hold a candle to Google when it comes to search results.

Nearly ten years ago I received an email from a former boss. He said I should check out a new search engine called Google. "Google", I thought, how odd. So I went to the site and saw an even less crowded screen than today's version. My first searches were so "right on" I never looked back. And guess what, so have hundreds of millions of other people searching for "stuff" on the Internet. My old search engine, Yahoo provides search results I can only call "interesting". I do a Yahoo search about once a year and quickly return to Google. Microsoft's Bing is actually quite good. Their results are far better than Yahoo's however there are so many tools that work with Google I have never made the permanent jump to Bing. As Microsoft and Yahoo start to merge search operations as 2010 starts it remains to be seen how things will turn out. I suspect the sum of the two will not be greater than their two parts.

So what, you say! Well I'll tell you what. Nearly 65% of users on the Internet search for goods, services and information using Google. Whether your business is a brick and mortar pet store in Spokane, Washington, a wedding favor web store based out of Christchurch, New Zealand, a non-profit organization in Columbus, Mississippi or a CPA firm in Toronto, Canada potential customers and clients are searching for **you** and the goods, services and information you offer! It is in your best interest for these customers to find **your** presence on the web before they find your competition.

That is what this book is all about, being found first in search engine results for your information, goods or service. Regardless of your technical background this book provides practical advice for your web site and your web presence.

This is obviously a hard copy book (OK, it's a paperback). There are a number of references to various websites throughout the book. Obviously you can't click on these links. We have created a page on our website with live links to make things a little easier to check out these great sites.

You will also find lists of useful tools. These are third party software tools that may make some of the tasks we talk about in this book easier to perform, especially if you have more than one website. Most are free, however some cost up to about $100. Check the webpage listed below for direct links to these tools on our site:

www.practicallocalsearch.com/seobooklinks.

You can also do a Google search for any of the software tools we list.

So let's jump right into the world of search engine optimization. It's not all smoke and mirrors and your efforts will surely lead to increased business over time.

Good luck and thanks for reading this book!

Practical Local Search

Local Search Marketing and SEO Consulting

Bellevue and Seattle WA

www.practicallocalsearch.com

Contents

Forward

It is really difficult today to make a small business stand out from the larger businesses. The small business owner has to leverage their web presence using innovative and highly targeted strategies so they can carve out a market niche of their own. With small marketing budgets and limited resources businesses have to find highly effective cost conscious methods to reach their target audience.

To be competitive on the web a business has to conquer at least a corner of the search engine and carve out their niche as their own. The best way to do that is to have a highly optimized website and a real plan for finding where potential customers 'hang out' on the web. Getting 'found' is the name of the game and search engine optimization (SEO) is part of a game winning strategy especially for the small business owner. SEO can be a game changer that helps not only increase a company's overall web presence but also to convert visitors to your site into customers. At the end of the day, that is how the ultimate measure of a website's success.

This book leads any business owner (large or small) through the process of understanding how to optimize a website so it increases the opportunity to build a real rapport with a potential customer base locally or globally. Using some simple on and off page SEO techniques will move a page toward that all important first page ranking for highly targeted keywords. The first page of a search term is generally the only page people search when looking for specific information regardless of the strength of material on page two. Human nature is that which is easiest and most obvious to obtain is often 'good enough'. You can't afford to languish on page two or beyond. With over 70% of all inquiries and searches conducted on line, it is even more critical for local businesses to have a strong viable competitive online presence.

Getting found on the most critical channel – search engines – is huge in business today. You have one shot to get found by prospects. B2B, B2C, no matter what you do as a business, your online presence must work for you. Consumers today do not rely on just word of mouth or print to make purchasing decisions. They often know more about the deals your company offers than the sales reps on the floor! People are doing their homework and researching goods and services on line before they spend. To be competitive you have to feed them valuable and actionable information. But first they have to find your website!

It is amazing how many small business owners see SEO and the web as 'voodoo magic'. Watch eyes glass over as you talk about optimizing a profile on any social media platform. It does not have to be that way. This book gives you what to do in simple easy to do steps. There are real implementable things you can do today for your site to start really building your presence online today.

Small, medium, and large businesses are all seeking inexpensive highly effective methods for tapping into the market and getting more business in the door. There is not as much disposable income around as there was in recent memory. In order to thrive in a contracted economy business must target niche buying audiences who are geographically close to a business' goods and services. For brick and mortar businesses this is even more critical. To make the market work better businesses have to be in front of that buying audience. On page and off page SEO is critical to that process but can be so overwhelming to consider. This book breaks down easy to implement elements of solid SEO techniques in step by step usable chunks.

Starting with how to build a local presence Rich and Shannon have created actionable material that brings valuable information and useful techniques for SMB's. If you are in retail, automotive service and supply, a restaurant, or local consultant you need to own your local presence where your shop, your store, and your customer base 'hang out'. Larger companies struggle to get more buying public through the doors and into a store. Value at a local level is huge! Having a local presence is critical to success and is now a tremendous struggle for many well established businesses.

Local search technology is growing and changing rapidly. Hyper-local services are pushing out to you via your computer, your GPS, and your mobile phone. They are driving potential customers to you, your business, and your social pages. It is fast, it is dynamically changing, and it is often in real time. Is your business plugged into the technology yet? Can you get found on Google Maps? Bing? Yahoo? City Search? Yelp? Local search is now the corner stone of a small business' web presence.

Often businesses have multiple locations across the country. Each location opens channels of social media like Facebook Fanpages and Twitter pages. How do these businesses make all their internet presences align to the corporate brand image or identity? How do they stay on message yet remain authentic? Get Found Now Search Engine Optimization Secrets Exposed is a great resource for creating not only B2C channels but B2B channels as well on LinkedIn with specific techniques and strategies for groups, questions, webinar postings, whitepapers, etc. No longer can B2C's afford to continue embracing the perception of LinkedIn is not a viable resource for their web presence as well. Everything has changed. You have to look at all the resources available and find where your potential customers are 'hanging out'.

This book is different from a lot of the books recently published on the topic of SEO. Get Found Now presents the basic theory behind the strategies and techniques in straight forward language free of the heavy terminology and acronyms found in so many technical books today. This book gives you what you need to know as well as how to implement the suggested changes. This is information you can act on immediately and make happen on your own. The high level actionable strategies and techniques included in this book will benefit any local or national business or organization.

If you are in business you need this book to make sure you get 'found' by your potential clients and customers and beat your competition to the top of the search pile. The internet can be the great equalizer for small businesses. To get found you need to be on the first page of search results. You need this book to get found. You can no longer afford to let your web presence grow by chance. If you want to target where people are researching and making their buying decisions you and your business should reap the benefits of

Evans and Geasey's work. Hurry, if you don't your competition surely will be studying this book.

Mike Lewis is the Vice President of Marketing at Awareness, Inc. He's a classically trained marketer and active social media enthusiast, proud husband and father and, an OBSESSIVE Boston sports fan. You can find him on Twitter @BostonMike or on his blog Social Episodes (http://blog.socialepisodes.com).

Overview

Are you tired of your website sitting around not attracting any attention or delivering any business to you? Would you rather it work for you by delivering customers and sales to your business? It is easy to make your site attract traffic and rank well in Google (and other search engines) if you follow the suggestions in this book.

Do you have a website covering a fairly popular topic such as iPods? If so, you'll have a lot of work ahead of you. However, if you are focused on a specific niche or product or you have a locally oriented business (contractor, professional service, store etc.) then you will do quite well following the included techniques. Later in this book you'll read about how to research and discover profitable niches.

Most companies and web masters simply do not bother to do the basics when it comes to website optimization. It's to your advantage when this is the case. Most of the suggestions contained here will be simple to do and in most cases free or inexpensive to implement (except for your time). This is especially true in less active niches or localities!

We are not search engine optimization experts; however we have been in technology marketing and consulting for almost 25 years. This book contains summarized ideas, techniques and suggestions we have researched, recommended and used with success.

Anyone reading this guide will discover more than one useful technique. To quote a popular legal disclaimer though, your mileage may vary! Please keep in mind that no one technique or effort will lead to success by itself.

Developing your site is an ongoing effort and you will integrate many of these techniques over time. Don't dive in and do everything over the weekend and become so overwhelmed you quit. It's a journey, and you will revisit some of these destinations more than once.

Enjoy yourself as you watch your creation grow. When you see your site moving up in traffic, your Page Rank move up a notch, or see your site ranked first for a good solid keyword I guarantee you'll feel great!

This Book Is For

This guide is primarily designed for small business owners with a web site they use to support their business. You could be a store owner, professional service provider or an online marketer. While the advice is targeted towards smaller web sites the techniques discussed here will provide effective results for more substantial web sites as well. Even if you have a small website for a side business or hobby you will find plenty of actionable techniques.

Many small business owners see optimizing their web site akin to black magic. It does have a bit of that but frankly it's easier than working on your car! If you have built your own site then it will be quite easy to implement these suggestions. If you have contracted with a consultant, friend, family member or student then pass this along to them with your suggestions. There is a action guide at the end of this document to track your progress or to give to your web site designer.

What Is a Search Engine and Why Do I Care

All I hear is search engine, search engine and more search engine! What is it and why do I care. A search engine is a web based application that finds information on the web for you. When you type a search query like "hunting rifle" the search engine looks through its database to find the best match for your keyword.

Search engine companies are focused on providing search results that provide the <u>best possible</u> match for the user's search. To create this match the search engines "crawl" the web with automated search robots to determine what is on each and every site on the web. A big job you say? Darn right, there are over a billion sites on the web! When a search robot visits your site they try to determine what it is about. They store this information and the engine creates a profile of your site. When a search query is entered for something like "hunting rifle" the search engine looks in its database and finds the site it feels best matches the profile of "hunting rifle" and displays it first in the natural (sometimes called organic) search results of the search engine. If you're number one then good for you!

All of your efforts in search engine optimization are focused totally on setting your site up as the number one site for your selected keyword phrases. In essence when someone types "hunting rifle" you want your site to be the one Google, Yahoo, Bing and many others think is the best site on the entire web for "hunting rifles" (or whatever your targeted keyword phrases are).

How Does Your Site Rate Today

It's always important to know where you are before starting out. Two basic metrics of website success are Google Page Rank (PR) and Alexa traffic rank. While neither is a definitive gauge of success both provide an indicator of how you stack up against your competition.

Alexa page rank is simply a measure of your traffic. The number one traffic site is Yahoo and it goes down from there. You can check out your site's Alexa traffic rank by going to Alexa.com and typing your (or any other) URL.

You can also get the Alexa toolbar which displays at the bottom of your browser and shows the traffic rank of any website you visit. Any ranking under 100,000 and the site is doing extremely well, under a million and the site is making excellent progress. Over five million and the site basically don't exist (for the most part, more on that later). Alexa stops tracking at about twenty million.

Alexa Tool Bar (Bottom of Browser)

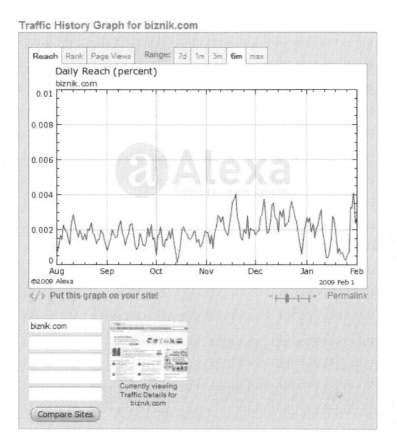

Alexa Traffic Data Page

Reach for Biznik.com: ⑦			
Percent of global Internet users who visit this site			
Yesterday	1 wk. Avg.	3 mos. Avg.	3 mos. Change
0.0027%	0.0024%	0.00215%	▲ 36%

Traffic Rank for Biznik.com: ⑦			
Alexa traffic rank based on a combined measure of page views and users (reach)			
Yesterday	1 wk. Avg.	3 mos. Avg.	3 mos. Change
41,099	45,455	47,549	▲ 16,851

Page Views per user for Biznik.com: ⑦			
The number of unique pages viewed per user per day for this site			
Yesterday	1 wk. Avg.	3 mos. Avg.	3 mos. Change
3.8	3.4	4.41	▼ 0.7%

Biznik.com users come from these countries:

United States	79.2%
India	7.0%
Canada	2.4%
United Kingdom	1.5%
Australia	1.0%

More biznik.com users...

Biznik.com traffic rank in other countries:

United States	14,298
Canada	43,384
India	52,165
Australia	96,514
United Kingdom	148,104

More biznik.com traffic rank...

Alexa Data Page

Now don't obsess over your Alexa rank if it appears low (a higher number). There may be some good reasons for this. One of your best gauges is how well your competition is ranked. If you deviate significantly from them then you'll want to get cracking! Are you outside of the US? If so your traffic is likely to be less (especially if you have a local domain like .ca, .com.au, .co.uk, etc.) simply because there is less traffic in your region. Lastly, your particular product or niche may simply have a small amount of traffic. This is why should compare yourself to your competition to validate where you are. Remember, it's just a guide!

Google Page Rank is an indicator of how "relevant" your site is. We liken it a bit to being part of the cool crowd. If you met someone at a party and found out Bill Gates thought that person was cool then you are likely to think so too (OK, maybe Bill Gates is not the best example of cool, but work with us here). If you found out we thought they were cool, you'd likely say, "big deal" (unless you knew us and then it'd be OK, but stay with me).

It's the same with Page Rank. The more cool (relevant) sites linking to your site the "cooler" your site must be. Get a few high page rank sites to link to your site and you are in good shape. To view the Google Page Rank of any site download the Google toolbar. The Google toolbar offers a lot of other great features and installs in a few moments. You will see a little slide graph that shows any page's Page Rank.

Google Toolbar Page Rank Icon

The importance of high Page Rank links to your site cannot be overstated. It is far better to have a few high Page Rank links than having a lot of lower Page Rank links. It's basically a logarithmic thing (like the Richter scale for earthquakes). A PR2 site is five times more valuable than a PR1 site; a PR5 is five times more valuable than a PR4. I think you get the idea!

Like the Alexa traffic ranking be careful of obsessing over your PR. A high PR helps you rank higher in natural search results; however, I have seen some very successful sites with a PR of 0 (zero). Again, see where your competition is and see how you do compared to them. Regardless of how your PR turns out any effort you do to improve it will pay dividends in your search results.

Now the sure fire indicator of web site success is where it appears in a Google search for your targeted keywords. If you appear on the first search page then you can forget about an Alexa rating or Google Page Rank! And if you appear in the top five or six, congratulations on a job well done.

Note: Throughout this guide I refer to Google. With well over 60% of search traffic you should expend your energy to maximize your results there. The good thing is your efforts there will also pay off for other search engines such as Bing and Yahoo.

How Does Your Site Rank in Search Results

Another key performance metric (the most important metric) is where you show up in a search on Google or any other search engine. The goal of course is ranking number one. In some cases this is very doable; in other cases simply being on the first page is more than adequate. If you are not on the first search result page but found on the second page then for all intents and purposes your site does not exist. Nearly 90% of those who search never go beyond the first page to view results.

So, do a search on your primary keywords and find what page your site shows up. See what your ranking is (not your Page Rank) and record it to measure your future progress. As you find your site take time to check out those that precede your. Take the time to view these sites, which ones look good and which don't. In most cases, especially in smaller niches you will be able to easily out shine your competition.

For really competitive market segments you may need to reduce your ambitions. If you expect to rank well for a term like "mortgage refinance" good luck. You will need a lot more than this book to do well. However for the target audience we wrote this book for we believe you will find an excellent chance for success.

That pet store owner in Spokane, Washington can easily beat his local competition, so can the web site owner in New Zealand, the non-profit in Columbus can easily rank at the top and even though CPA is a high volume keyword they can rank well if they use focused keywords and apply a little effort.

In the following example I have highlighted the three areas of a typical Google search results page.

- On the right side is a list of sponsored or paid listings. The top of the screen has another set of paid listings.
- Below that is a short list of shopping sites with the items from the search query.
- Below that are the results of natural (also called unpaid or organic search) search selections.

In this case the search term is "mountain bike" which is pretty generic; in fact there are over four million sites with the exact phrase of "mountain bike" in them.

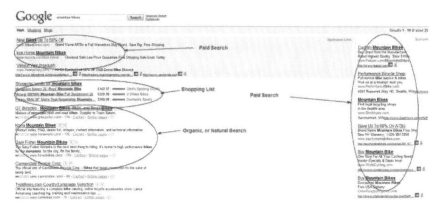

A Typical Google Search Result

This is a fairly typical result. Whatever Kona Mountain Bikes is doing they should be commended! They are ranked number one for a fairly competitive keyword (and a generic one at that) and are not forced to spend money on pay-per-click advertising. If you happen to be a mountain bike dealer I'd examine every last page of their site to see what they are doing!

What's the Purpose of All of This

Why do you want to bother with all of this? When someone types one of your keywords in a search engine, you want your site to come up as high as possible on the first page of Google or any other search engine. You also want this to happen while spending as little money as possible. To make this happen you must increase the exposure and effectiveness of your site on the web.

Enhancing your exposure is a holistic project. You will be doing a variety of activities all working together to improve your web presence and ranking. They will all be explained later in this guide.

Making Your Site Stand Out and Be Noticed

There are two ways for your web site to move up the traffic list and improve your Page Rank (and improve your Google search placement). The first is called "on" page efforts and the second method is "off"page efforts. These techniques are generally called Search Engine Optimization (SEO). Yes we know the first thought you might have is "this is like having to work on my own car, why would I ever want to do that". Frankly, our first thought was pretty similar to that. However, we think you will find this to be a lot easier than you thought. Read on and you will find nearly two dozen ways to improve the performance of your website.

This guide is meant as a basic overview of things you can do to improve the performance of your web site. For virtually every section we could write dozens or hundreds of pages in painful detail (and many have). This guide provides only the basics and some additional resources for those who wish to explore the concepts in greater detail.

"On" page efforts include maximizing the use and presence of keywords on your web site. There are a few things you can do that will result in the majority of the effect (this is the case where the 80/20 rule is still valid).

"Off" page efforts are those that point other sites (and viewers) toward your site. These efforts will be seen by the search engine robots and help elevate the relevance of your site (and its Page Rank). Both "on" and "off" page efforts will result in exposure for your site and it working its way up to number one.

You Are Number One, Now What

Your site is ranked number one for your search terms, now what? You need to be clear ahead of time about what you want to accomplish when a person arrives at your site. There is only one reason for most of us doing this; making money. There are many sites that exist to simply provide information; in that case it is still helpful to direct people to your site. However, for most of us we have a profit motive.

This guide is not going to address what you should do once a person arrives at your site. We are going to focus on how to get the visitor there in the first place. Visitors will arrive in two ways, from the results of a search (in most cases from Google) or they will arrive from another site that has a reference to yours.

Note: This guide focuses only on Search Engine Optimization (SEO). SEO is the process of maximizing the visibility of your site using the techniques in this guide (and many other techniques not mentioned). There is also a technique known as Search Engine Marketing (SEM).

SEM is the process of using monetary means to direct visitors to your site. This is basically Pay Per Click which requires using tools such as AdWords. SEM techniques are not in this guide. For most businesses (especially local businesses) you will not need to expend any resources on SEM as your SEO work will put you on page one of Google.

Keywords

Search engines are driven by keywords. Keywords are essentially the words people use to find you and what you are offering. It is crucial you know what your keywords are for each of your web pages. There are numerous tools for determining keywords and they are all fairly easy to use.

When people begin their search for information on the web they usually start with a general category and then refine their search with more specific search terms. For the most part one word keywords are too general and should never be used to plan web site optimization strategies.

Let's use the word "mortgage" as an example. Do you think you are going to be the number one site for mortgage without spending large amounts of time and money? Not likely.

Now, for something like "seattle 5.5 percent refinancing" you are likely to have more success. Generally when people use a one word keyword to search they are looking for general information. When people use phrases they tend to be looking for specific information relating to purchasing something (or paying for the information they find).

Knowing the keywords your customers use to find you is absolutely the most crucial thing to do in this entire guide. If you use the wrong key words you are wasting your efforts. Some of your keywords will be quite intuitive and easy to figure out. Others related to basic keywords may take a bit of research and testing to determine.

One way to determine effective keywords is to see what your competition is using. The way to do this is to go to the website of your top competitor (or the top ones in your selected field). After you are at their web site select 'View' and then select 'Page Source' from the browser menu.

A new window will open with the background code for the web page. Look for a listing called meta keywords. These are the keywords the site owner is highlighting. See how they stack up against yours. You will also find in many cases the site owner does not even have keywords listed. If so, all the better for you! If you find your competitors do not have any keywords listed then smile. They are going to be easy pickings!

```
<meta http-equiv="Content-Type" content="text/html; charset=windows-1252">
<meta name="Keywords" content="dentist, Belltown Dental, Christine Shigaki, Dr. Shigaki, Dr. Chi Hsiao, Seattle dentist, Belltown dentist, tooth, teeth, restorative dentistry, preventative dentistry, cosmetic dentistry">
```

Meta Keywords (viewing Page HTML Source Code)
View This at Your Competitors Site

One word of warning on keywords, ensure they are useful! Forget throw away words like quality, number one, welcome, robust and other empty words. They are worthless when searching. Business names, unless well known are not helpful either as people do not normally search on names. If you use your name as a search keyword on your site you are wasting your efforts. Don't be offended; just remember you should use keywords your potential customers will use. Keep one thing in mind, only your momma cares about your name and your business name! Your potential customers only care about what you can do for them!

Now that's not to say you shouldn't use your name or your business name on your web site. However you will want to focus your efforts on your primary search keywords. As you read through the following sections about on page optimization you will see this a little clearer.

One last thing to keep in mind when developing your keywords is related words. You will have a group of keywords and phrases; however, potential customers are an unpredictable lot and could in fact use other similar words to find you. Google has many useful tools that will help you find related keywords. The Google Sets tool will allow you to search for these related keywords. As you implement the strategies and tactics in this book consider including these additional keywords in your content to help corral those unpredictable potential customers.

Google™
Sets

Predicted Items
road bike
mountain bike
bicycle
bicycle part
bike rack
bike part
biking
vermont
bike trails
mtb components
bike riding
cycling
mtb parts
performance bicycle
exercise bike

[Grow Set]

Google Sets Example (mountain bike and road bike keywords)

23

Keyword Tools

Google Keyword Tool- It certainly can't hurt to use this free tool from the number one search engine. This should be your primary keyword tool.

Google Insights- This is a good tool for comparing keyword traffic by geographical area. Enter a keyword and you can select a global, or by country display of where the keyword is performing. While we are not discussing Pay Per Click advertising this is a great tool for that.

Google Sets- This helps identify additional keywords associated with your primary keyword selection. See the screen shot above.

Google Trends- Another in Google's keyword research toolbox is Trends. This tool analyzes one or more keywords and plots their performance over time. This is great for determining the seasonality of your selections.

Keyword Elite- This is a very full featured tool to research, analyze, and find keywords. Their site has an extensive library of videos to you help you maximize your research. This is one of the most popular tools for keyword research and very reasonable in price. It is the companion product to SEO Elite which I will highlight later.

Wordtracker- This is the most popular keyword research tool for active Internet marketers and webmasters. It is however fairly pricey. This is a link to the free version.

On Page Optimization

There are seven things we suggest to improve your on page optimization. All are quite easy to figure out and only take a few minutes to implement. Amazingly you will find relatively few web sites (especially for smaller niches and businesses) implementing all of these suggestions. To make these changes you or your webmaster will need to edit the HTML code of your web page.

Most HTML and web page development tools have forms for you to enter the information I discuss below. You can also use your HTML editor and directly enter the information in your source code. For those of you using the WordPress Content Management System (CMS) add the All in One SEO Plug In (free). It will make implementing some of these suggestions a two to three minute effort and pay huge dividends.

It is quite easy to spy on your competition and see what they are doing. When viewing a web site simply select View, Source and a separate window will open and you can see exactly what they are doing in regards to some of the following techniques (see the image earlier in this guide). Remember, it's not stealing it's research!

One important thing to keep in mind as you read about page optimization is it is focused on a *page*. Unless your website is very small (one to five pages maximum) then you will want to optimize each individual page on your site. While this may sound like a pain it is important. Each web page may have a different focus, or display a different product. For example if you own a pet shop you'll want to have a set of keywords for cat products, dog products and bird products. One set simply won't do. You'll either have too many related keyword phrases per page, or not enough.

Your Web Page Title

The web page title is what appears along the top of your web browser. The title information is also what the search engines will show as the blue bolded text people click on to arrive at your site. If you do not enter anything in the title field it will display the name of the page taken from the URL. For example if the page URL is www.website/page 1.html then the title will say "page 1".

It's in your best interest to have something more informative than that! In fact, this is one of the easiest and most effective changes you can make to optimize your site. Best of all it is very quick and easy to do.

Title at Top of Browser Bar

Title in Google Search Listing

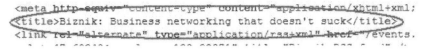

```
<meta http-equiv="content-type" content="application/xhtml+xml;
<title>Biznik: Business networking that doesn't suck</title>
<link rel="alternate" type="application/rss+xml" href="/events.
```

Title in HTML Source Code

Each individual page should have its own title tag. This allows you to maximize the exposure of the keywords essential to each page. At a minimum create a title tag that provides the keyword(s) for your site or the selected page. The length of the title should be less than 65 characters. Google seems to max out at 65, while others allow more.

Effectively use your keywords and keyword phrases in the title but don't be repetitious. Separate keyword phrases using the | character (SHIFT \). Take some time to think this out and it will pay dividends. Be sure to mix in location keywords if it makes sense. Use model numbers if a specific product is listed on a page. Always remember to consider how your potential customers might find you, your products, your cause or service. One other little trick is to position your most important keywords at the beginning of the title. Play around a bit with the order and flow to get it just right and it will pay dividends.

Meta Tags (Keyword and Description)

In years past using meta tags was one of the most effective means of optimizing your site. No longer, search engines are smarter than that. However, we maintain this is still a useful exercise. It helps crystallize in your mind what the keywords are for each page, this helps guide how the page content should be optimized. Also, some search engines still evaluate sites for meta tags so it pays to do every little bit.

There are two meta tag fields you should be concerned with: description and keyword. As with the title take advantage by optimizing the meta tags for each page on your site.

The description meta tag is shown on a search results page underneath the blue bolded title text. If there is no meta tag information this area will be populated with text from the page with varying results. Personally, I suggest this is the place for your elevator pitch. Make it short and snappy (with keywords) and someone seeing your search result will know exactly what you offer. Your description tag should be about 150 characters long.

In some cases Google will reach into your page description and extract text and display that on the search results. It is important that the first one or two paragraphs on a page are well written and contain your keywords. You will also find when your description is displayed the keywords the searcher used are shown in bold.

HTML title tag
Definition and Usage. The <title> tag defines the title of the document. The title element is required in all HTML/XHTML documents. The title element: ...
www.w3schools.com/TAGS/tag_title.asp - 30k - Cached - Similar pages -

Meta Description (Notice Highlighted Keywords)

ADA.org: Find a Dentist
Catalog, |, Find a Dentist, |, Seal Program, |, Contact ... Find a Dentist. You searched for and Your search yielded 0 results. ...
www.ada.org/public/directory/index.asp - 21K - Cached - Similar pages -

An Example of a Poor Use of Meta Description

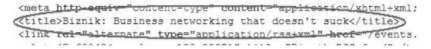

```
<meta http-equiv="content-type" content="application/xhtml+xml;
<title>Biznik: Business networking that doesn't suck</title>
<link rel="alternate" type="application/rss+xml" href="/events.
```

Meta Description Source Code

The keyword meta tag is where you will place the relevant keywords for the page. Don't repeat yourself here, this is not a time when one is good and two or more is better. Search experts feel that from seven to ten keywords or keyword phrases is the maximum for each page. If you serve a local area be sure to mix up keywords related to your business as well as including your location identifiers (main city and one or two close by cities or communities).

```
<meta http-equiv="Content-Type" content="text/html; charset=windows-1252">
<meta name="Keywords" content="dentist, Belltown Dental, Christine Shigaki, Dr. Shigaki, Dr. Chi Hsiao,
Seattle dentist, Belltown dentist, tooth, teeth, restorative dentistry, preventative dentistry, cosmetic
dentistry">
```

Meta Keywords in Page Source Code
Notice Use of Business and Location Keywords

There is "controversy" about whether to include meta keywords or not. Google has stated publicly they do not place a high value (or any value) on the use of meta keywords. In the past webmasters would fill the meta keyword section in with dozens (or more) of related (and sometimes non-related) keywords in order to influence the page rank. Google of course wised up to that practice!

We suggest using meta keywords, in a case when all things are equal the inclusion of meta keywords might tip the scale in your favor. We also find it useful to understand exactly what keywords are in use for any single page. Lastly, some search engines such as Yahoo (and some feel Bing) still consider meta keywords.

Heading Tags

Headings are similar to chapter and sub-chapters in a book. On your web site you can assign attributes to selected areas of text. Attributes are things like bold and underline. In this case you assign an attribute of H1 (or other heading levels) to a line of text. In most cases this makes the text bold and larger. It will also surround the selected text (in the HTML code) with H1 tags. This is a key to the search robots that this is important text. Headlined text normally appears as bold in your content and in a larger type size.

H1 Heading Tag

As important text this is closely examined by the search robots. Because of this ensure your headings have your keyword phrases. You can also have subheadings (and sub sub-headings) with H2, H3 and so on attributes. Frankly, an H1 tag and one or two H2 tagged headings per page is adequate.

Alt Tags

The Alt tag is applied to images you embed in your site. As you insert an image on a page you will have an opportunity to enter a short description of the image. You don't need an entire sentence, a short keyword phrase will normally do is actually better for SEO purposes. Make sure each image has a unique alt tag. Alt tags can be important to a site with a lot of graphics and less text. For businesses like designers and artists there may be a large number of images on a page. Mix up the keyword string for each image and this will help considerably.

Another advantage of using Alt tags is your images will be picked up in Google (and other engines) image search functions. At the top of a search results page will be a selection for image search result. On this page will be images related to your keyword search. If you actively use Alt tags your images may appear on this page. The result of this is a viewer may click on your image and the page this image is displayed on will be presented. It's a bit of a back door entrance to one of your web pages.

Google Image Search Result

Intra Site Links

It is a good idea to link between pages on your web site. Using keyword rich anchor text (see the section Off Page Optimization for more details on this) with links to other pages will help boost the presence of your keywords to the search engine robots. You don't have to overdo it, a link or two a page is all that is needed.

Another good practice is to have a site map. For many web site development tools this page is automatically created for you. When a search robot visits they find the site map and this page shows the robot where everything is and how the site links together. For WordPress users there are a number of nifty free plug-ins that does this for you quickly and easily.

Also, a good practice overall and for search engine ranking is the addition of a Contact and Privacy page. There are plenty of good examples of Privacy pages on the web, just find one you like and make the changes you need for your site. I know, most people never read this but it shows the search engines you are serious about your site and your visitors.

On your Contact page you can put an email address, phone numbers, Skype contact, a map, directions, social networks, and anything else you think is useful. If you have a lot of sites you can reuse this time and again.

Keyword Density

The last thing to do is to focus on the density of keywords on your site. Avoid the urge to simply load up your page content with keyword phrases. The search robots are smarter than that. Your content should read as if a normal person wrote it.

When I researched what ought to be a good percentage of keyword density on a web page I got a very useful answer: Look at your competition and do slightly better than they do. To check on your competition check these tools out.

Keyword Density Tools

Keyword Density Analyzer- A great free tool for search engine optimization and internet marketing experts.

Keyword Elite- Mentioned this great tool earlier; this tool will also help analyze your site and your competitors for keyword density.

Content

The last on page technique involves creating content that is interesting useful information. Search engines look for content and use the existence or lack of it in judging a web site. Adding content to your site is one of the most important things you can do over time to get and keep your site ranking at the top.

To generate and use content see the different techniques in the off page optimization techniques listed below. The other major advantage of having useful content is users will want to come back! If you have visitors who come back often you will continually have the opportunity to sell them more products or services. They will also be more apt to sign up for your newsletter (if you offer one).

Remember these are the two goals for getting someone to your website, capture their email address and/or sell them something.

I will discuss the creation of content a little later in the guide under the Article section.

A Note About On Page Optimization

This book has only touched on the basics of on page optimization. Within each of the techniques there is considerable fine tuning you can do. The selection, order and placement of your keywords can influence your success. If you need to take your site to the next level I suggest you engage a local individual with experience in search engine optimization. However, you will find for smaller niches the topics we have covered will provide you with a considerable edge over nearly everyone else.

Off Page Optimization

Off page efforts are designed to position you and your site as an authority and worth exploring. Primarily you will place articles, press releases, forum posts, social media profiles, directory posts, videos and links on complementary sites around the Internet.

When you do this you will have links to your site in the placement. As these placements grow the links pointing to your site will help your web exposure and ranking. One of the key elements in search engines deciding if your site is an authority (cool) site (and ranking higher in Page Rank) is the number of links on the web that point towards you.

Imagine for a moment if Bill Gates listed your web site on a web site of his. Do you think that might generate some activity on yours? Of course it would. So you will be looking to place all of these cookie crumbs around the web leading visitors (potential customers and viewers) to your site.

There are eight strategies you can use. You can do each of these yourself without cost. However there are resources and tools making the process easier and more efficient. You can also make use of third parties that can help for a small cost. Listed here are a number of free and paid tools. If you are doing one or two sites then the free tools will be more than adequate. If you are doing more than one or two sites then you'll definitely want to look into the paid tools.

With all of these strategies you will want to embed your website URL, a short description of your site (quite possibly what you used for your meta description tag) and your name. Normally this will be in the form of a signature block at the end of the document (article, press release, video, etc.). Two key things to keep in mind as you add your URL to various places:

- Avoid using the phrase "click here" with your web site URL linked to the word "click here". The phrase "click here" shows up in 1.5 billion sites (yes that's with a B).

- Always create your link using *your site name* www.yoursitename.com or have a short site name and add the link URL to that. The underlined text is called anchor text. It is helpful to always have this as keyword rich as you can, no matter where you are placing links (on your site or others).

Press Releases

The press release is a specifically formatted and written document you submit to free or inexpensive public relations related sites. The press release is designed to highlight a particular event at a business or organization. It could be to announce the release of your web site, signing up a new important supplier, an event and so on. Make the press release about something interesting to someone. Editors in all types of media are dying for new content and someone may pick up your piece.

Most media websites (newspaper, radio and TV stations) are well trafficked and have a high Page Rank because they are relevant. By picking up your press release they may edit it a bit, but they will keep your contact information intact. You now have a link from a well trafficked, high Page Rank site to your site. Google will think you are cool! When you complete your press release think of where you want to release it. You can of course use the larger free-for-all public relations sites and you are likely to get some results there. However, be sure to target local sites and resources as well.

Did you win an award or are opening a store, alert your local paper. Launching a new web site or releasing a product then alert publications in that industry. Don't go overboard. If you are doing these more than maybe a half dozen times a year then you are doing it too often. Sure IBM can crank these out all the time, but they have a lot going on. Do a press release on something of note and you will get exposure. Be sure to put all of your press releases on your website, you never know when someone will pick one up and publicize it.

If you are not familiar with writing a press release then I don't advise doing it yourself. There are some rules to the formatting and basic layout. I suggest getting a contractor to do it for you. Use eLance.com and publish your job for as little as $50.

Press Release Tools

Media Syndicate Submission Service- This is a free press release submission service. All press releases are reviewed by human editors prior to posting, so be aware it may take a few days to a week for posting. If you like the services they ask for a donation.

PRWeb- If you are serious about using a press release as a tool then this is the place to go. It is not free, prices range from $80 to $360 depending on the degree of exposure you want. This is a high Page Rank (7) and high traffic site (9,100 or so) so this will provide a boost to your site.

Articles

The use of articles is an excellent way to get exposure for your site and demonstrate your content expertise. Articles generally take the form of "How to", although you can write about pretty much anything that relates to your site topic.

Articles should be in the 400 to 500 word range. You are not writing *War and Peace* so keep things focused. Try to pick about five topics of interest to your readers about your subject matter (your niche).You can write the articles yourself or contract them out. You should be able to get an article written for about $5. You can easily find an author on eLance.com, or check out Textbroker.com. Textbroker.com charges by the word and level of quality.

For a one star quality article the cost is a dime a word, $4.00 for a four hundred word article! I personally would use the two star quality level at 14 cents a word. Frankly, at those rates it's not worth your time to do it yourself. Keep in mind your article is not the place to sell or promote. It is to inform. The process of selling will take place after a person gets to your site. You want to position yourself as a knowledgeable person regarding your field.

Once you have your articles you will post them on your website (remember search engines love content) and then on article directories. There are hundreds of article directories and they are just what the name implies. There are directories hosting thousands (or much more) articles. They are categorized by subject for easy searching. Once you select an article directory, select the appropriate category and post your article. When you post an article you will have the opportunity to list your personal or company details. Enter your name, company name (if appropriate), email address and most importantly your web site URL. Once your article is posted you now have another link to your site!

Leonardo Wood specialises in teaching website owners how to do their own SEO.

For Instant SEO Tips to Help You Get Your Website on the 1st Page of Google click: SEO Tips

Article Source: http://EzineArticles.com/?expert=Leonardo_Wood

*A Nice Example of an Author Signature Line
and Effective Use of Anchor Text Links*

Most importantly, ensure the title of your article is keyword rich. When your article is listed the title you use will be part of the URL for the article. This example: http://ezinearticles.com/?Five-Natural-Ways-to-Eliminate-Panic-Attacks&id=1969113 shows how your title will appear. This is a very specific keyword phrase that will appear high up in Goggle when someone searches on it. Ensure you put the effort in to maximize your article title.

While there are hundreds of article directory sites as with everything on the web only a handful are worth posting to for the purpose of link building. Be careful when doing a lot of posting, there is a point where too much is bad for you. The search engine robots don't like a lot of duplication. So if you plan on doing a lot of posting consider having two or three variations of each article prepared and mix them up (do not put variations of the same article on a single article site).

Once your article is posted to an article directory members of the directory are able to take your articles and post them on their own site (you can do this for your own site as well to get started with other articles). You must list all of the author's information and maintain any links. The great thing is you now have another link pointing to your site! To maintain freshness you may want to consider slowly posting your articles. If you have five to ten done when you start your efforts try and post them over a few weeks. Then over time add a new article every month or so. Search robots love fresh content!

Be sure your articles support the keywords you are focused on. Over time as you collect more and more articles you can make a set of them and offer them to websites complementary to yours. Once they are on the site they will provide more inbound links to your site. Remember to create an effective title; it will help in ranking high in keyword searches in the search engines.

Ezine Articles, One of the Top Article Directories

Article Submission Tools

Article Submitter- This tool automates the article submission process allowing you to quickly complete what can be a fairly long task. It also has a very nice video instruction library.

Content Rewriter- This is a cool tool that lets you take an article (or any content) and have it slightly rewritten. This makes it easier to submit to larger numbers of article directories without having issues with duplicate content.

SEO Elite- This is the program I use to submit articles. While costing more than Article Submitter Pro it really does a lot more. It will also help with link submissions and analyzing your competition. This is a great tool! Also consider purchasing Keyword Elite along with it. It's the best one two punch for maintaining and creating web sites for profit.

Article Directories- Some good directories are:

- Ezine Articles
- Go Articles
- Free Ezine Site

- Article City
- Article Alley

Testimonials and Endorsements

Testimonials and endorsements are great techniques as they are a sneaky way of getting your links out there. A testimonial is a statement about someone else's product, service or web site. They are usually a couple of sentences to a paragraph long and also provide the opportunity to place your name and web site URL after the testimonial.

If you are indeed an authority in your field offer to do product endorsements or evaluations. If you use a particular product then offer the manufacturer a short endorsement (with your link in it of course). While this particular method will not work as well as others when you do get the opportunity you are likely to get some good exposure. Some people who started doing product reviews have created some lucrative web sites and blogs (plus they get free stuff to try out and keep).

Videos

The use of videos is a relatively new option. YouTube.com is by far the most popular and highly trafficked video sharing site online. Basically it is an article directory, but with videos. It's a little more free form but nevertheless a library of videos. YouTube (and most of the video directories) is a bit of a mish-mash of submissions. There is plenty of opportunity to make use of these heavily trafficked sites. You do not have to stick with only YouTube, there are plenty more, but don't overdo it.

The purpose of video submissions is creating an inbound link and creating interest in your site so a person clicks on your link. As you might suspect there is a lot of junk on YouTube, and most people are simply trying to show off their creations. That's OK; it leaves lots of room for serious folks to shine.

In order to make the most of your video submission record a decent video. You can purchase a digital camcorder (even one with 720p HD) for a little over $100. Use adequate light and ensure the sound is recorded properly. Just doing these simple things puts you're ahead of most everyone else on video sites.

Keep your videos less than two minutes, anything longer and viewers lose interest quickly (actually a minute is better). If you have a company logo use it as a fade in and fade out image. You may want to consider adding a watermark throughout the video with your URL (keep it small though).

Background music or sound effects tracks add a lot to the quality of a video. However, be certain your music is not copyrighted! If you start having some success with a video you don't want it pulled because you are using a copyrighted work. There are plenty of sites with royalty free music for free or a small purchase price.

When you setup your account be sure to completely fill out the profile. Viewers will see this when they view your video. You can also enter your website URL, this is important as it's the whole point of uploading your video.

As you prepare your YouTube posting be sure to name the upload file with a keyword rich file name, not something like "video1". Add keywords to the video title and add keywords in entry fields for your video. Ensure your YouTube account (or channel) has a good descriptive name, a good keyword rich description and most important of all, your domain name!

The last thing to consider is adding videos to your website. Embed the video image on your site and the search engines will see this as new content. There are dozens of video sites other than YouTube but that is the best place to start.

As a quick example we had a bad storm in Seattle in late December 2008. As a lark I went outside and shot a short video of the conditions and posted it on YouTube. I just wanted to forward the link to a few friends and YouTube is a great place to host it. Well, less than 48 hours later it had nearly 150 hits! I basically did nothing and people were looking at it. Imagine if you were really focusing on results with your site's keywords and a targeted video.

Video Tools

Video Submitter- As with articles if you are going to do this frequently you will want an automated tool. This will submit your video to YouTube and many others.

Forums

There are thousands of forums on the web about nearly any topic under the sun. A forum is a free-for-all of discussions about all subjects related to the forum topic. Forums are huge in the Internet marketing world. While this is an effective venue I would make this a little further down on a "to do" list.

Forum marketing takes time. You cannot simply drop into the forum and start selling. You need to spend time on the forum and start making a contribution to the discussions. As you build up some history you can start making hints about your site and what you have to offer. As we discussed earlier in the section on articles be sure to have a signature block with your site description and URL.

One thing to watch about forums is the tone. By that I mean some forums can be negative, they are just one big gripe session. Check the forum out for a bit and if it looks as if this is the case move on. Find one that is positive and spend a bit of time on the site once or twice a week. After a few months you can start making some moves toward self promotion.

Forum Tools

Forum Submitter- This tool will automate forum submissions and save you a lot of time.

Link Building

We have discussed a number of ways to simply get one way links into your site. With link exchanges you will engage with other sites to share your links. In other words, it is a case where they display your link on their links page and you do the same for their site on your links page.

First, you will want to have a links page on your own site. This page will display all of your link partners' links. I suggest breaking the page down into categories to make it easy for viewers to find useful links.

You need to first locate complementary sites, especially ones with a high Page Rank and encourage them to link to you. You can do this manually but it will take time. SEO Elite is a useful tool which will easily locate potential link exchange sites and allow you to quickly exchange links with them. The other avenue is to hire someone to do this for you.

The first step is to identify the link partners you want. They will include complimentary sites, sites with an associated focus, and any other sites that might be identified. One way to identify sites is to see who comes up when you do searches with all of your keywords. You will also want to look for link directories. These are sites that are essentially sites of links related to certain topics. You can find these by searching Google with your keyword and the phrase directory.

Another great technique is to see what your top competitors have as link partners. Using Yahoo Site Explorer you can identity sites with links to a selected domain name. Once you find these link sites follow the steps listed.

Next you will take all of the links to these sites and enter them on your link page. Create categories of links and begin populating the page with the links, and a short description for each one. Even in smaller niches you could have dozens or more. Make it look sharp! Next take the list you developed, sort it by Page Rank and start at the top. Find an email address of a contact on the site and send them an email. As you approach each potential link partner you tell them you have placed a link to their site on your site and you would like them to do the same. Be sure to send a personal email message, not a mass mailing. Focus on what your site offers to readers of their site. Never suggest if they ignore you you'll remove their link.

Include in your email the exact placement you would like. Your linked text should be your site name using your prime keywords. The description of the site should closely match what you use for your meta description. Link building takes time and it should be measured out over weeks or months. If one day you have ten links and the next 100 Google will get suspicious. Just have an even pace and your site will move up steadily in the rankings. Over time be sure to track your links to be sure they are being maintained on other sites. Some sites will go away, others will remove your link and other calamities will occur. Persistence and perseverance is the key to back link building.

Another way to build links is to allow your site visitors to add your page to different social bookmarking sites. There is a very nice utility called "Add This" that is popular. By adding a few lines of code to every page on your site you make it easy for your readers to bookmark you. It's free as well!

Add This Bookmark Utility

Link building is the best thing you can do to build up the search profile of your site. Take a long term approach and over time your site will grow in strength. A key advantage of strong back links is it is very difficult for your competitors to gain on you. Remember, this is the hard part of SEO but pays the greatest benefit!

Link Building Tools

SEO Elite- This program submits requests for links. It also does a lot more. It will also help with article submissions and analyzing your competition. This is a great tool! Also consider purchasing Keyword Elite along with it. It's the best one two punch for maintaining and creating web sites for profit.

Link Submission Service- This is a standalone link submission service that works well.

Blogs

Web logs, or blogs are all the rage. A blog is a web site in the format of a dairy or journal. The site publisher adds content to the site and categorizes it for future recall. Posts don't have to be long, maybe a hundred words or so. However, they should be frequent.

Personally when I arrive at a blog I check the date of the last post. If it is more than a month or two old I figure it's out of date. It's easy to become a slave to your blog! To keep it active and interesting to both your visitors and the search engines you must have new content constantly and consistently.

The upside is if you have an active blog you can create plenty of internal links from your blog to your site. This will help the performance of your site.. If you have a site and want to have a blog I don't suggest having it hosted by Blogger or other free services. These free services do not rank as well with search engines. A common method is to create a sub-domain for your blog (www.blog.yourdomain.com). A sub-domain can have a similar look and feel to your company website or be completely different. For WordPress based sites your blog is an integral part of the site, this is the best option of all.

Other blogging strategies include offering to contribute articles or reviews to other blogging sites related to your web site's subject. Every active blogger faces the same issue of continually providing new content so you are likely to find many opportunities to be a guest blogger.

The opposite works just as well. Be open to having guest bloggers, the interaction of a few of you between each other's sites over time will benefit all of you (and ease the writing anxiety on occasions).

Blogging Tools

WordPress Goldmine- We are big fans of WordPress. It's really the platform you want to base your blog on if you are going to be serious. This guide will really get you started.

WP-Robot- This is a new tool we recently found. It provides for automated postings of RSS feeds, articles, Amazon products, YouTube videos, eBay listings and a few other types of dynamic data.

Social Media and SEO Opportunities

A large-scale social media (or call it social networking) presence will give you great search results if you create an effective profile using the right keywords. Most social media sites have a powerful search reach and rank high with search engines. If you and your company name are on the major social media and networking sites you stand a good chance of placing high in search results for relevant keywords you use in your social profiles.

Search engines are constantly on the prowl for related content for each search query. They are also looking to eliminate duplicate content when ranking material to return to the person conducting the search. To help ensure your content is unique make sure to vary the content of each profile, while still focusing on your most effective keywords. Keywords play a huge role in both your profile content and your profile name and in SEO. With the advent of real-time search, social media and keywords are even more critical to SEO for your business.

The world of social media and networking sites is exploding so fast it's hard to keep up. Every social network site offers some benefit; it's just a question of how it impacts you. Don't just sign up because someone says it's a good idea.

The three most popular ones at the moment are Facebook, LinkedIn, and Twitter. At the end of the day all three of the sites are there to create links and exposure for your main site. Before you embark on a journey into the brave new world of social networking be sure to understand who your customers are, where they hang out and how they interact with you.

The following sections focus on using these three social media sites to help enhance your overall web presence. They will deliver traffic to your sites and provide another web venue to educate and direct visitors to your site. Yes, social networks can be a bit of a time suck, but effectively used they will benefit your own personal and company exposure on the web and your site's.

Twitter

Whether or not you are a fan of micro blogging you need to at least consider the potential of using it for SEO purposes.

Twitter can be an excellent link building tool for your site and with search engines like Google adding real-time search capabilities you can't afford not to make sure you take advantage of optimizing your Twitter presence. We are not suggesting using Twitter to let your followers know when you have a cup of coffee of take the kids to the Y for a swim. This is a strategy to enhance your reputation and lead interested visitors to your site.

Tim Tebow Crying After Losing To Alabama | Entertainment News For ...
Dec 6, 2009 ... **Tim Tebow Crying** After Losing To Alabama Hahaha From: vikingguy2 Views: 0 0 ratings Time: 00:47 More in Sports , Internet News, ...
netchex.com/tim-tebow-crying-after-losing-to-alabama - 1 hour ago -

Twitter / Kristin Johnson: Aww **Tim Tebow's crying** on ...
Aww **Tim Tebow's crying** on senior day. I might too. #gogators.
twitter.com/KSuzJ/status/6150110110 - Cached

The Official **Tim Tebow Crying** Thread - MWC Message Board
4 posts - 3 authors - Last post: 6 hours ago
The Official **Tim Tebow Crying** Thread: Please post any pictures you find!
www.mwcboard.com/www/forums/index.php?showtopic... - 6 hours ago -

Google is already indexing Tweets as evidenced by tweets showing up in Google's first page of search results. You can and should use Twitter to build more high ranking links on search engines. If you are not Tweeting already and do not have a Twitter account you should create an account with a Twitter username that is easy to recognize and relevant to your brand/company. This username is your custom URL on Twitter. For example:

twitter.com/shannonevans
twitter.com/localsearchsea
twitter.com/write4women

When you create your twitter username you are creating an address for future search engine indexing and promotion on other web platforms. Make sure your username reflects your brand, promotes your name or makes use of your keywords (global or local). Use the variation of your name that gets searched most according to either a keyword search or the analytics on your website or your local search business listing.

Add your domain name to your profile and then optimize your bio box to include more keywords related to the benefits you bring to your customers. The bios placed on Twitter profiles are indexed by search engines and so there should be some relevance between the content you tweet, the content in your bio and your website. Remember for most everything in Twitter brevity is not only a virtue but a requirement.

Once your Twitter account is up and running you can build some links to your website on your Twitter profile. Your website URL in your Twitter profile promotes your website to your followers and drives traffic back to your site.

On your website you should place a "Follow Me On Twitter" button somewhere relatively prominent on a page where your customers are most likely to see it. Integrate your Twitter URL in your global footer (your web site should have a footer on every page with your site URL and other linkable information). This is what appears at the bottom of every page on your website. This helps your Twitter URL rise in search engine rankings.

Search engines are looking for relevancy and authority. Generating valid followers and inbound links improve your authority. So does having your content re-tweeted to the rest of the Twittersphere.

What you tweet is important to your followers but the first words of each tweet are what matters for SEO. Those lead 42 characters in your tweets become the title tags in a search result on Google (This includes your username). The entire tweet gets indexed by search engines but the key to SEO relevance are the first characters of each tweet and impact its value. In fact in most instances the lead characters in SEO should be your most valued keywords.

shannonevans
8:05pm, Dec 05 from TweetDeck

Local Search and Geo located Tweets...oh the power of Twitter and Google combined! Bwahahahahaha...http://bit.ly/7h6b0J

Local Search and *Geo located Tweets* are keyword phrases that are often searched on Google. Using good keywords that are often searched and related to your content is really important when trying to get your work indexed. Writing keyword rich tweets when possible is critical to SEO. Buzz words should only be used if they are pertinent to your followers and add value to your content. Leveraging your content with keyword phrases makes the search engines return to your tweets and index them.

Using URL links in your tweet to drive users back to your content on your blog or website is good practice too if you use a URL shortener like Bit.ly or BudURL. These track click-throughs for each link you shorten. They can aggregate the links and track them over time.

A Shortened URL

This tracking data lets you know what content has been most popular and most often clicked through. The links themselves do not add to your search strength. Unfortunately links on Twitter are what are called 'nofollow' links. Nofollow links do not pass on the link strength we discussed earlier. This is typically done to battle spammers from creating content simply to link to lousy sites selling Viagra, mortgages and the like. Search engines do however index and pass on the Page Rank of the original URLs.

Google and Yahoo completely eliminate the links from their ranking calculations. MSN/Bing just ignores your links, but Ask.com seems to allow them. While Ask.com does not own a huge corner of the search market, 200 million+ search queries a month can't be ignored! So keep linking because it obviously does not hurt your search ranking either!

Twitter is a great way to use SEO to drive more traffic to your site, your blog, and your business so you can ultimately gain more customers. SEO is about adding onsite and offsite promotion opportunities for your site. If you provide good content on your Twitter site that sends your followers to your website you are creating an exterior link. That generates metrics that search engines seek for ranking factors: number of unique visitors, number of page views, time on site, etc. Generating traffic to your website from Twitter will result in improved Alexa rankings and greater Page Rank and move you closer to the top of organic search returns.

Facebook

Can Facebook help your SEO profile? Can you truly optimize your business Facebook fan page for search engines? Yes you can!

Facebook allows businesses to have a vanity page on their social networking site. It is a great place to create a hub to other information about your company or your brand or to create links to other sites that are related to you. It is different from a personal page as it should be representative of your company and your brand and not your personal life.

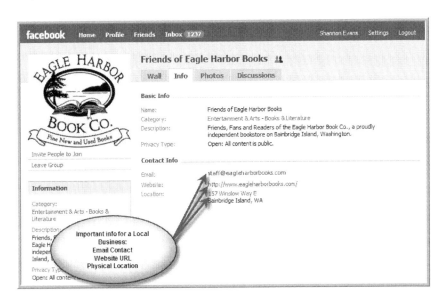

The first step to optimizing your site for search is to identify the best keywords you should use (have you heard this before). Keywords should be selected on the basis of how potential customers who have never heard of your brand name but who need or want your goods, products, services and information. Keywords are tricky to pick out but with a little help from Google's keyword tools (see the Keyword Section earlier in this book) you can uncover not only the right words and phrases but the search volume itself. Try and find good keywords and link them to your company name as you choose your Vanity URL.

Make sure your Facebook Page URL represents the identity of your business and your brand. They frown on black hat behaviors so keep it above board and choose a username that represents your brand! Part of the process to get a vanity URL is to have 100 fans on your page. Once you get more than 100 fans you can implement this SEO element with Facebook.

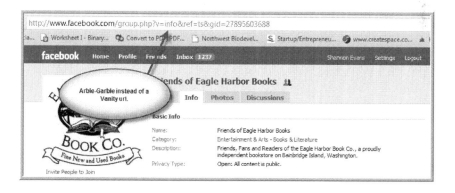

Once you have investigated and selected the best keywords and selected your vanity page URL it is time to concentrate on the actual optimization of your Facebook page. Here are some general guidelines for on page optimization:

- Add keywords to your "about" box
- Place your company website link URL in your profile
- Add more than one URL, include your Twitter link, LinkedIn profile link, etc.
- Publish interesting content on a regular basis that is related to your products or industry that is not 'salesy'
- Use keywords in everything you post if possible
- Be social, interact, evoke comments
- Add video from YouTube, add photos or products, your store front, etc.
- Find links related to your site content.

- Put your Facebook page URL on your email, newsletter, website, etc.
- Be personal, it's not all business after all just don't be too personal!

The "About" text is the place to pack your description with keywords as close to the top of the page as possible. You are limited by the amount of text you can place in here but it is still the best place to add custom text. There is a 250 character limit so use highly selective keywords in your text!

The "info" tab is a critical place to include more keywords/phrases as well as your links to your website and other social networks where your brand has a presence. This is essentially where the descriptive metadata for your fan page is pulled by the search engines and really boosts your content score.

Facebook has a high page rank with all the search engines therefore it is critical to have your website listed on your Facebook page to provide this valuable link. To have your website displayed on your main profile page access the information box on the left side of your profile page. Click on the yellow pencil and you will be able to edit the box. Check the box "website" for your site to be displayed. Now visitors can go directly to your website. Here are some things to add to this box:

- **Local Search Information–** Complete address for a brick and mortar business or city, state, and zip code if you work from home or only have PO Box.
- **Company Data–** Mission statement, Products, Services, Brands carried

- **URL**– add links to your website, blog, and other social networking personal pages

Facebook lets you create "static FBML" (Facebook Markup Language) boxes and tabs for large volumes of content, images, or video. The more content you have on your page the greater your content density score with Google; however, keep in mind that each tab you create has a separate URL from the search engine perspective. To add a custom tab or box to your page:

- In the search box on the top right of your Facebook page type in "static fbml"
- You will go to a page of listings. Select the "Static FBML" application button.
- A new page will open and on the top left side are two options. Click the "add to my page" icon.
- Choose the page where you wish to add the custom content box or tab.
- Close the dialog box and go to your Fanpage. Just below your profile photo click "edit Page"
- A new page will open. In the application list is the application "FBML 1." Click on the pencil beside it.
- Select "edit"
- A new page will open with 2 fields - "Box Title" and "FBML". Name the box or tab with a Keyword related to the content you will place there. If this will be a Tab Title you will be limited to 10 characters.
- Click "save changes"
- To return to your application settings page click "edit" at the top of your page.

- Click the pencil next to the name you selected for the FBML application and then choose "application settings."
- To add the FBML you just created as a box select "add" next to the "box" option.
- To add the FBML you just created as a tab select "add" next to the "tab" option.

Status updates are a great place to post direct links to your website; however, you want to do that judiciously. No one likes to be sold to or constantly pitched. Since Google really likes pages that link to relevant sites, posting relevant related links near the top of your page's structure are legitimate Google boosters for your Facebook page.

Post the raw URL in the status update frame or use the "attach link" feature. Posting the raw URL Facebook automatically links the text to the URL. The resulting anchor text is what it is, you can't change it; however, the URL is linked directly to the destination page and does not have Facebook.com as part of the menu bar on the destination page.

If you use the "attach link" feature Facebook pulls the title, body, and any images from your page and creates a suggested image and text to the side of your page's link. This is great for increasing your keyword density too by changing the anchor text before "sharing" your link. This link will go through a share URL that places the destination URL in an iframe that has the Facebook menu bar at the top. It will also include a share feature as well as a place for comments.

Content is still king so what you post beyond URLs can influence your searchability. Highly optimized keyword rich content is useless if it is not interesting and varied. Photos are terrific but add keyword rich captions perhaps with a geo-targeted keyword for additional search opportunities. Post an event and include text and keywords as well. Create a discussion forum for those events and to discuss brands and product reviews, etc. All the content you share on your Facebook pages is indexable by search engines.

There are even some offsite things you can do for your Facebook page. One of these is getting inbound links from you website and vice versa. Reciprocal related linking from related and authoritative websites help your Page Rank.

Put a Facebook badge or Facebook Fan Box widget on your website to encourage your website followers to link back to your Facebook page. Links from other Facebook pages are also a form of inbound links to your page. The more fans you have the more links you have to your Facebook page thus adding to your overall search presence.

Encourage your followers to comment and discuss topics on your page. Get them to "like" content on your page as that links their name back to their profile page thus creating yet another back link. When fans comment back on your page from their Facebook account, Google sees their entry as a reciprocal link. This increases your 'footprint' on the web. Reciprocal linking is heavily weighted by some search engines.

SEO is important to all that you post on the Internet related to your business. Growing your social media connections on

Facebook is greatly aided by simple search engine optimization tactics. You can do a lot to maximize your brand's exposure to search engines through your Facebook Fanpage.

LinkedIn

LinkedIn is the granddaddy of business networking sites. With nearly 50 million users around the globe it is <u>the</u> business networking site.

LinkedIn has great authority with Google and other search engines so why not use it as another source of SEO links? Where do you begin and how do you tap into LinkedIn for some SEO strength? Let's start with your profile on LinkedIn and the website links you can add there. Creating unique anchor text links to your website on your LinkedIn profile is easy to do and provides a 'dofollow' attribute that is invaluable if your profile has content relevant to your website's content. Adding your name to your LinkedIn profile URL adds to the search friendliness of your name. To create anchor text links to your website on LinkedIn select "Profile" on the left side of the home page.

A new window will pop open and with a tab titled "edit my profile."

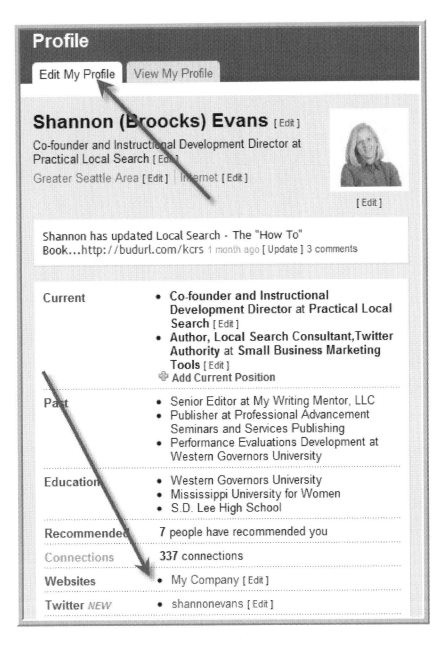

Scroll down the screen to where lines "Website" and "My Company". Select the edit button. A new window opens and there are several pop down menus. First select "other" in the website bar, then to the right type in the keyword rich name of your company or business followed by the URL where you wish people to land first. Then scroll to the bottom of the page and select "save".

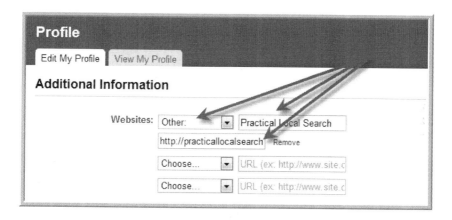

You can add three up to three URLs so add your blog and maybe a second website for your business website and a third for your business Facebook Fanpage. These are all live, direct, 'do follow' links which are happily scanned by the search engines! Using the "other" selection rather than the default selection allows you to add relevant anchor text which then adds to your link strength.

Make sure you also set your profile so that your public view exhibits your website and adds to your Page Rank. To do this go to the bottom of your "edit my profile" page and select "edit" beside "Public Profile." Editing your links in this fashion is seldom done by even savvy LinkedIn users so take advantage of it.

Current	• **Co-founder and Instructional Development Director** at **Practical Local Search** [Edit] • **Author, Local Search Consultant,Twitter Authority** at **Small Business Marketing Tools** [Edit] ✛ Add Current Position
Past	• Senior Editor at My Writing Mentor, LLC • Publisher at Professional Advancement Seminars and Services Publishing • Performance Evaluations Development at Western Governors University
Education	• Western Governors University • Mississippi University for Women • S.D. Lee High School
Recommended	7 people have recommended you
Connections	337 connections
Websites	• Practical Local Search [Edit] • Practical Local Search Blog [Edit]
Twitter *NEW*	• shannonevans [Edit]
Public Profile	http://www.linkedin.com/in/pshannonevans [Edit]

This will take you to another page where you can select what the viewing public can see. To get the most "bang" for the search engine optimization buck select "Full View Recommended" and fill in all the dots but most importantly the "website" button.

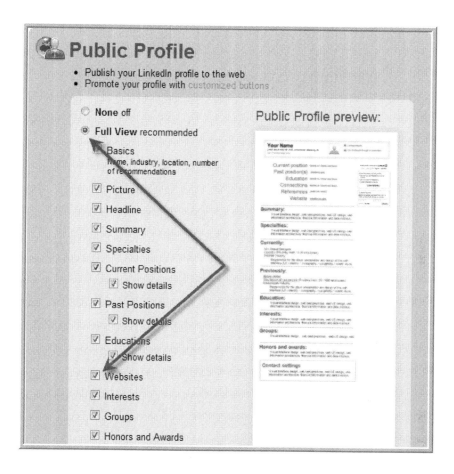

This will help your profile get indexed by the search engines and your website collect a Page Rank influence from having your profile page on a high authority site (LinkedIn).

Now let's shift attention to the actual contents of a profile. First and foremost the use of relevant keywords is critical to the process! The headline, personal interests, summary and job description should be populated with keywords related to your website or blog. Avoid keyword stuffing but do utilize important words that are relevant.

Headline– While this is such a small piece of information it is really valuable as your headline is what shows up in lists, groups, and email updates. It says in a nutshell what you do and what your position is. Optimize your job title using your highest ranking descriptive relevant keywords. Instead of stating your title as "Marketing Manager" use "Internet Strategist Manager" or "Social Media Marketing Manager" for better leverage. Avoid throw away words such as *experienced, savvy, veteran* and other modifiers. They offer no search value and waste space better used for quality keywords.

Current– This segment cannot be technically 'edited' as it is pulled from the "I currently work here" from your experience list. It can be optimized for search if you make sure the description of what you are currently doing is keyword rich and relevant to your website. Pay special attention to your current job title as that is what shows up first on your profile!

Summary and Specialties– Use keywords relative to your website to explain what makes you different or what makes you stand apart yet are related to your brand/industry. Provide product, service, and consulting details that help someone make a decision whether they want to connect with you. Avoid empty words like: *quality, fun, innovative, significant,* etc. They add no search value. You can either list your skills or you can create a descriptive paragraph of your specialties. Avoid pasting your cover letter and resume in this section.

Experience– Provide a rich keyword description of your current job. Elaborate in detail on your responsibilities and current work. Your previous position descriptions should be brief but also filled with keywords that sell your current expertise and add to your credibility.

Connections– It is interesting how adding connections on LinkedIn improves your website's SEO. It improves your personal visibility online as well as your website's and your blog's visibility.

Groups– Joining groups that are industry related helps you get found by others. Participation in the groups helps draw attention to you and your company.

Answers– The answers section of LinkedIn allows you to not only improve your reputation it also allows you to construct internal links to your profile which provide more "go juice" for your profile in search engines. These pages are indexed and so are returned by search engines in their search results. The answers you provide create another opportunity for your website to get exposed as you will add a link to it or your blog in your signature line of your interaction with those who are seeking your expertise or who are reading your answer.

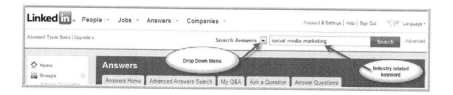

LinkedIn is an incredibly valuable SEO resource for you just waiting to be tapped. All it takes is a little time, some good keywords, and persistence when building a network of connections. If you build it and tend it carefully, 'they' will come (search engines).

LinkedIn by itself is a powerful tool you should take advantage of and use to promote your expertise as well as your web presence. With the added bonus of providing valuable links to your website don't miss making the effort to optimize your profile.

Social Bookmarking

Social Bookmarking is a rating tool site visitors use to share their favorite websites, blogs, articles, and web content with others. This social aspect makes bookmarking a terrific way to promote a business to a highly targeted niche audience as part of a social marketing campaign.

What is social bookmarking and how does it work? Social bookmarking is when a user creates a bookmark that tags a website with keywords and sometimes ratings that are user created and shared with others in a bookmarking site. Social bookmarking lets users organize and categorize internet resources as well as provide differing perspectives on content. This creates a collaborative content filter on another website resulting in excellent website promotion for your content.

The beauty of social bookmarking is that content posted on a social bookmarking site that is highly relevant and resonates with readers can spread like wildfire on the internet. Social bookmarking of your web content, blog posts, and articles can result in a highly effective cheap marketing method to reach your target audience. If you find the social bookmarking sites that provide "dofollow" for your links you can rapidly build your web presence and promote your business.

Social bookmarking helps search engines find and rank content that is 'tagged' by users. If you provide opportunity for readers to easily bookmark your content you will build links faster, increase web traffic and improve your Page Rank as well.

The more you submit fresh relevant content with links to your site to social bookmarking sites the greater the likelihood of attracting a steady stream of qualified leads and customers to your site. The more people who share a website's link the greater the webpage's ranking with the search engines. Most of the social bookmarking sites have a high link value with the big three search engines (Google, Bing, and Yahoo).

When you create a social bookmark to your page or article you also create an external link to your website or blog. Make sure you use relevant keywords in that link. If someone else bookmarks that same page they are also creating one way links and that increases your site's ranking with search engines. There are many social bookmarking sites to choose from to help your search ranking:

- Digg
- Del.icio.us
- StumbleUpon
- YahooMyWeb
- Furl
- Reddit
- Blogmarks.net
- Ma.gnolia
- Spurl
- BlinkList

Don't forget to use social bookmarking to comment on other related sites. A well placed relevant high quality keyword rich comment with a link back to your site can be just as important for SEO and someone linking to you. Aside from the longevity of your site and onsite SEO techniques, getting back links from high authority sites is the primary way to attain high rankings. Without links to your site you can't stay in the rankings even with great keywords and continually fresh keywords in most cases.

When creating your web site be sure to add the tools to allow your visitors to easily add your site or page to one of the many book marking sites. For WordPress sites there are dozens of plug-in tools and most are free.

What If I Have a Physical Location

If you have a brick and mortar location such as a store, restaurant or professional service there is one other tool you should use, local search. One of the most frequent search patterns is for local goods and services. People may search for *Seattle dentists*, *Anaheim car washes*, *Boston hair dressers* or millions of other similar type searches. To assist visitors with these types of local searches there is local search in Google, Yahoo and Bing.

Local search is a tremendous addition to your website SEO efforts. An effective local search profile will lead potential clients and customers directly to your website. You will use some of the principals you have learned already in this book.

Local Search

In most cases the search engine knows where you live (your computer IP address gives you away) so it assumes you mean the location closest to you (it knows if you live closer to Arlington TX or Arlington WA for instance). These searches will occur in the basic Google search function as well as in Google Maps. The results are a bit more complete in Google Maps, however you should use the same due diligence to create your business entry regardless of the search origin.

Once you have entered the search you will be shown a list of businesses in the location you specify and in the case of Google a map with their locations pinpointed. Now, here is where it is up to you to generate success. You should immediately go the Google Local Business Center (this is free) and enter your basic business information. You will have to verify your information with Google either by phone or a paper postcard.

Google Local Search for Seattle Dentists

The great thing about this is you add all of your physical location data and you can accurately position the Google map pin right where your business is. Another very helpful feature is the ability to add categories. Here is where your keywords come in to use. If you are a dentist what are your specialties; pediatric, cosmetic, elder care etc. All of these can be searched locally (such as *Seattle pediatric dentist*). If you are a restaurant list specialties or regional cuisines or a dish you are popular for preparing. I like pot stickers so I'd love to be able to type *Seattle pot stickers* and get a list of places with pot stickers. Fortunately I can, but the list's not very complete.

You can also add pictures to your listing. This obviously helps as a picture makes you stand out. However, it can also make it easier for a visitor to identify your establishment as they look for it when they come to see you. Take a look at this great example of search on *steakhouses in Boston (go ahead and check out the local search listing by typing that search stirng and checking Google Maps)*. Makes you want to go get a steak right now doesn't it! You can add up to ten pictures.

You may also add videos to your local listing (it refers to YouTube). This is another great opportunity to present your business. You can use your YouTube videos and make them do double duty, or have some that apply directly to your business.

Lastly, and I think quite ingenious is the ability to add a coupon. If a potential customer sees a number of listings and yours has a coupon you are much more likely to get the visit or business. Be sure to consider this option when creating your business listing if it makes sense. This is very seldom used.

As an added note even if you are not a local business but just a local branch office it makes good sense to add this information so clients and customers can easily find you in any town you have a physical presence. It is common for people to search for a company office when trying to locate it. Searching Dallas Frito Lay when traveling to Dallas should bring up all the information a visitor would need. It's a great touch to help interested visitors find you.

I mentioned earlier in this guide that for smaller niches the "quality" of websites is such that you can easily out market them. In regards to Google Local Search you will find it even easier to dominate your competition. Be sure to have an accurate listing and map location, a good photograph of whatever you think sells your business and a coupon if appropriate. And lastly, make good use of applicable keywords when entering your business information. This will greatly increase the likelihood of your business being found when local searches are done. If you have multiple locations do this for every site.

Before we leave this section we should mention again what an incredible way to market your business this is. You do not even need a web site! The real secret here is that local search results are posted before organic search results or are within the first couple of listings! In the standard Google search screen local search results are at the top of the page along with the map locations. Your competition could use every technique listed in this guide and you could not even have a website and you could be listed above them! Take the time to do this right and might very well own the listings related to your place of business in your town!

Oh, and just to remind you this is free!

Bing and Yahoo each have a similar service. Yahoo has three levels of service from free to $25 a month. The basic (free) listing is useful enough. Paying a monthly fee is crazy when Google is free and provides about six times the search traffic! Bing offers a free service but it is only active within the Bing maps section. Frankly, when using Bing it is not hard to understand why Google is so much more popular. But...having your business listed in as many places (and for free) makes sense. It only takes five to ten minutes to do this.

Achieving Local Search Success

Every business wants to stand out by ranking well when a potential customer or client does an Internet search. Local search is now becoming the normal way potential clients and customers find a business to purchase goods and services. In fact over 65% of potential customers and clients use the Internet to find local goods and services. The following pages provide an overview of some of the key success factors you will want to consider as you refine and optimize your businesses web presence. Optimizing your local search listing will in turn help you with a stronger over SEO search footprint as search results will show in both the organize first page results as well as in the local search results.

Your Website Helps in Local Search Success

While you don't need a website to have a local search listing it certainly helps. Nothing fancy mind you, a short WordPress blog or a two to three page "brochure" site. Potential customers expect it now and the cost of entry and maintenance is so low it's absurd to not have one. Your web site will also help your local business listing ranking. Not by a lot, but as always when it comes to optimization on the web every little bit helps. Up to 15% of the success of a local search listing can be credited to your own website. So, while you can get ranked well without a site that extra 15% will be helpful. If your niche is fairly competitive then you'll definitely want to consider these tweaks to your site (or building your own site).

Some areas to consider improving on your site include the following highlighted suggestions. You will notice right off the bat the nearly common sense nature of these suggestions. Use the product or service and city name you want to rank for frequently. As an added bonus the work you do on your website to help strengthen your local search listing will help your site rank better in organic search. In fact, in smaller niches it is quite possible to rank at the top of local search as well as in organic search.

Full Address and Phone Number on a Contact Page- Every site should have a contact page. On the contact page be sure your contact information matches your local business listing.

Inclusion of City and State in Title Tags- The meta title tags on a web page still remain an important element of on page optimization factors for the page. Having your city and state name match that of what you want to rank well for in local search can help. If you want to rank for "Chicago CPA" then have Chicago in your title tags. Use city and state contact tags on all of your pages; you should at the minimum have them on your contact page.

Product Service Keywords in Titles- That same "Chicago CPA" should have the term CPA in his page titles (and other meta tags such as description and keyword) to ensure strengthening the site's SEO value.

Location Keywords in URL- If you are creating a new domain name (URL) for a business then be sure to utilize your product or service and your location. A domain name such as *www.chicagocpa.com* is helpful in both site SEO and your local search listing. If you already have a domain name then add folder names with your information. As an example *www.hastingsaccounting.com* could have a contact page called *www.hastingsaccounting.com/contact-chicago-cpa.html.*

Your Local Business Listing

In the first section we focused on your companion web siteit generates about 15% of the success in a local search. Up to

40% of the success of a well ranked local search may result from the completeness and optimization of your local business listing. This hardly comes as a surprise!

Carefully crafting your local business listing should be done only after spending time on some basic keyword research. If you don't know what your potential clients and customers are searching on to find you, you could waste effort. Be sure to understand the following:

- What cities where you wish to primarily rank.
- What product or service description where you wish to primarily rank.

Once this is complete perform some basic keyword research to see if your assumptions were accurate. On the home page of our site (www.practicallocalsearch.com) are a number of keyword research tools. Spend a little time and see how you did with your assumptions. Once this is done use your identified product and service names and your location names to craft your local business listing.

The following are some key factors in the success of your local business listing and how well it will rank for your selected keywords. It should be noted that some of these suggestions will not always be attainable. I'll note that as we proceed through each one.

Claiming Your Local Business Listing- Frankly, this is the most important action to take of all. If you don't own your listing then you cannot do any of the other actions recommended here. Worse, you are vulnerable to having your listing hijacked. Claim your listing today!

Local Business Listing Address in City Searched- This is one area where you cannot always have control. It's a big benefit to be in the city where you want to be found. However, that's not always possible. For more information on location see the section on location reference at the end of the document.

Use of Effective Local Business Listing Categories- Google offers the greatest flexibility here. Use your main and secondary product, service and location keywords here. Categories seem to be a powerful tool in search opportunities. You can create up to five in Google, just don't keyword spam in the categories. In Yahoo and Bing you have to use their categories and my observation is they are pretty minimal in effectiveness and variety.

Product or Service Local Business Listing Title- This is a key element in creating your local business listing. Use your business name, one or two product or service keywords and one or two location keywords to create a smooth sounding business title. This is a key element of search success.

Nearness to City Center- Much like having your address in the city where you want to be found there is not much you can do here in many instances. For more information on location see the location reference information at the end of the document.

Product or Service in Local Business Listing Custom Fields- Custom fields are different from categories. They offer a wealth of opportunity. Consider adding the following (or create your own):

- Specialties (another recitation of your products and services)
- When founded
- Certifications
- Brands carried
- Special equipment used
- Other keywords people may search on (very applicable in niche industries)

Local Business Listing with Local Area Code- In most large cities this is not a big deal. In the greater Seattle area we have three area codes. Seattle is 206, Bellevue 425 and Tacoma 253. It's not a big deal if they don't "match up". However, if you are in Seattle and your listing uses a Jacksonville, FL area code that is likely a bit of an issue. If you don't have a local phone number get a Skype number and forward it to your phone (about $60 a year). Google Voice is a new alternative. Google Voice provides you with a local number you can forward wherever you like and includes a number of voice services for free.

Local Business Listing Images and Videos- Images and videos add a great element of appeal and information to your listing. Until recently every listing for a "Bellevue art gallery" search did not have an image. That's crazy, they sell art! Yet, carpet cleaners had pictures. Use your logo, pictures of your building or product and your staff. In Google you can have up to ten, and three videos. Keep your videos short, maybe 30 seconds. Post them to YouTube and link them to your local business listing.

Offering a Coupon- In Google you can add a coupon. They appear to help slightly in boosting your search ranking. A new feature has added a link to your coupon, which will show up when someone searches on "location and product keyword coupon". It's an added bonus for search and potential customer's love a deal.

Each element of your listing adds to the overall performance of your listing in a local search. Hit all the bases and you'll be sure to have a home run.

Citation and Reviews

Reviews are a major tie breaker for local search listings. All things being equal more reviews, from more sources will help put your listing at the top and keep it there. It may also catapult your listing into the top ten where it previously was not found. Google likes to see there is interest in a business from the community. Additionally potential customers like to see reviews as the number one factor for many people is what other existing customers have to say about a business or service. Up to 30% of local search factors may relate to citations and reviews.

In most cases hospitality businesses and service providers will typically have existing citations in various locations around the Internet. Here are some of the directories where you will find reviews:

- Yelp
- Insider Pages
- Citysquares.com
- MojoPages.com
- SuperPages.com
- Yellow Pages

- InfoSpace
- Switchboard.com
- Ask Business Search
- InfoUSA Sales Solutions
- Localeze.com
- InfoUSA.com
- Citysearch.com
- AOLcityguides.com
- Superpages.com
- Switchboard.com
- Judy's Book
- Angie's List

In most cases these are legitimate reviews left by actual customers. In some industries there are marketing service providers that generate user reviews. I was told by a dentist their competitor used such a service to generate tons of reviews. I also know some businesses contract with service providers who go offshore (Philippine Islands mostly) and have reviews artificially generated. This is not a good practice in general and perhaps unscrupulous.

For new businesses and independent professionals you will want to develop a plan to generate reviews. Ask your friends to help get the ball rolling. Ask existing customers if they will help. Offer new customers an incentive if they leave a review. Make it easy for them to do this, provide specific links and instructions. Offering a bonus like a Starbucks gift card or a discount on future business will all help your efforts. Be cautious though, don't bunch reviews up at once, space them out. It looks odd if you get ten reviews one day and none for the next two months.

Citations are also like backlinks. Links in sites that have your business contact information also help the cause. Mentions in local newsletters, event calendars, media sites (radio, newspaper, and TV) will create backlinks and citation mentions for your local business listing.

Some important considerations in your review strategy:

Obtaining Reviews From the Major Directories- The list above covers most of the major search directories. There are likely smaller ones serving regions or individual cities. If you have a hospitality business (restaurant, bar, hotel, etc.) then you likely already have reviews.

Local Citations- Web sites that serve the local community such as media, Chamber of Commerce, city guides and so forth may have mention of your business or service. Be sure they have accurate links to you and contact information.

Reviews in Search Engine Listings- The major search engine local business listings allow you to leave reviews. This is an easy and convenient place to leave reviews if you are not in the hospitality or contracting business.

Customer Reviews at Third Party Websites- There could be hundreds of these in any locale. They may also include local blogs. Again, be sure your mention contains accurate location information.

Positive Customer Ratings- Oddly enough it appears that it does not really matter whether the reviews are good, bad or indifferent. This only applies in regards to the success or failure of the listing, not to customer's perception of your business.

A little time spent on cultivating reviews will result in big dividends in your search presence and success. Take a look at how many the first few local listings have. That will be your target to beat!

How to Lose Points in Local Search Success

It is possible to lose some points in the game, possibly up to 20% of your score by doing everything wrong here. The good news is you're not likely to do everything wrong or even come close if you follow the steps above and avoid the following ones.

Keyword Spamming- Keyword spamming is the overuse of your selected keywords. I have seen listings where the description and the categories are just keywords strung together. First, the search engines don't like this and penalize you. Second, it looks and sounds stupid. Remember, you are trying to impress a potential new client or customer so do so.

Multiple Addresses on Your Contact Page- If you have a number of locations create a separate contact page for each. Be sure to create keyword rich URLs and title meta tags as discussed earlier.

Negative Reviews- Negative reviews are not likely to hurt you in regards to your ranking success; however they may be a turn off for your potential clients and customers.

Exclusive Use of Toll Free Numbers on the Contact Page- It is very helpful to add a local number to your contact page(s) instead of just a tool free number. The local number adds, well a local flavor.

Multiple Local Business Listings with the Same Business Name- Now this is a big negative and is clearly spam. Ensure you have only one listing for each legitimate location. Anymore and it is clearly out of line and deserves a negative impact.

Exclusive Use of a PO Box- This is a difficult situation. For a variety of reasons you may only have a PO Box. If you are in that situation and you are not using an official USPS PO Box then call your PO Box a suite number.

Multiple Local Business Listings with Same Address and Phone Number- This is another harmful situation, however it can be problematic where you use a shared office situation. It appears that as long as the listings with similar addresses are not all yours then you are OK. If you are doing the work for other companies consider having different accounts for each listing.

Local search is a powerful tool for the savvy business owner or professional. Following the guidelines in this white paper will go a long way to getting you ranked at the top of local search results, and maybe organic search as well.

Location References

Generally the location being searched is the primary determinant of success in a local search. And why not, if you are looking for a business in Seattle, WA you are not likely interested in driving to Bellevue (or Dallas instead of Ft. Worth, and so on) to find what you are looking for. For most businesses (stores, professionals, contractors and others) who have been around for years, there is not much you can do to optimize your location, you are where you are! New businesses, however, may want to consider their location of record (license, mail delivery and website contact page) as part of their selection in where to lease or buy space.

While distance from the city center seems to be decreasing as a factor in local search success, the strength of the location in the search results poses a major problem for mobile service-based businesses who visit their clients, rather than having customers come to them. After all you don't visit the plumber to get your toilet unclogged! Adding to the issue is these mobile service providers are frequently in lower cost areas, or areas with more room for their equipment that are well outside the city center. Yet the businesses still do the bulk of their business in the city area.

The most popular way around this problem for the savvy business is to purchase a PO Box or UPS Store address in the cities where they desire to rank. There is some evidence this is declining in popularity, however it remains a technique that when coupled with optimization of the rest of your listing will result in success. As with most areas of local search just don't get carried away and open multiple PO boxes throughout the city.

Note: Using a PO box with a local phone number (using Skype for instance) a business can open a virtual location in another city and achieve search success. This is handy for service providers who want to open up new areas without actually establishing a direct physical presence.

City Search

Another resource is CitySearch. This site has separate cities for hundreds of US cities. CitySearch is a Yellow Page like directory. This, unlike virtually everything in this guide is a paid option. However I have found when searching for hospitality and retail services CitySearch listings are typically at the top of the heap. In fact (although I don't advise this) you can use CitySearch as your sole web site presence.

Like Google Local Services be sure to enroll. Add every piece of information you can (photos, videos, offers, promotions, directions, parking, hours, phone numbers, dress code, affordability, web links and menus). Next, get some reviews posted. Ask friends or favorite customers to do so. I'd also create a few different log in names and add a few of your own. Create some buzz! Also, keep an eye on your reviews, if the last one was six months ago then get some new ones added.

Go to the enrollment page and check out the Video link. This sample there is a fantastic example of using video to promote yourself, your site and your business. It's a minute long and really hits the high points.

One last interesting item is a list of the top searches on each city home page. Take a look at the search terms and see if you can use them. I was looking at Jacksonville when I wrote this and saw a top search term was post office. Well, maybe you are near a post office, or you can setup your directions to say how close you are to a post office. Try to use these terms in your CitySearch listing and it will likely help you out!

CitySearch is not the only site like this. There are other national sites and there are frequently regional and city sites (especially in larger cities like New York and LA). I suspect most of them are fee based as well.

Giving Your Site a Nudge

Whether you have a new site or an established site generating extra traffic is always a good thing. These techniques though should be used for very specific reasons. Generating traffic for the sake of generating traffic is a waste of your time and your visitors' time. If you have specific reasons for generating traffic then by all means use them. These techniques will generally be used by Internet marketers whose sites exist solely for generating income using a dizzying array of methods.

However you may find them useful for your needs. These needs may include promoting a new product or a popular hot product. You may have a new site and want to have a good number of new visitors.

This technique involves sending visitors to your site using classified ad sites such as Craigslist and USFreeAds or the link generating sites such as Squidoo and HubPages. Each site is well trafficked and highly ranked which helps your site back links as well. To effectively use this technique you will create ads on each site promoting your products. First create keyword rich title descriptions for your listing (where have you heard that before). Next create a quality description with photos and links to your site.

On USFreeAds you can have your ad active for about 45 days. Craigslist ads in large cities are active for seven days and in smaller cities for 45 days. Users finding your ad in either of the sites may click on through to your site. This helps traffic to your site and provides links to your site as well.

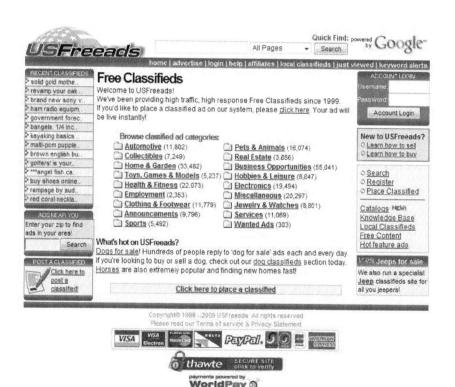

US Free Ads Classified Ad Site

Squidoo

Squiddoo is an informational user generated site where web pages are kept in a 'collection' of 'lens' that are publicly accessible. Anyone can create a page on Squidoo in less than five minutes; however, to do it in a way that drives traffic back to your website and builds back links will take a more concentrated effort.

Getting traffic from Squidoo back to your blog or website is not that difficult if you use good keywords in the lens' content and the title tags that are relevant to content on your blog or website. Squidoo lens are searchable and therefore are incredibly valuable for driving traffic back to a site if you include the all important link.

To build links with Squidoo to increase your rankings begin with the anchor text in the link. Carefully consider where the link point, where it will reside on the page, and the keyword rich content that surrounds the link. Implement deep linking on your lens as well. Link to your internal pages to promote your site so it is obvious to search engines. This not only increases your sites visibility on the web it increases the rankings of additional pages on your website. The beauty of a Squidoo lens is that you can create dofollow high quality keyword related links that will ultimately help your site achieve a higher PageRank.

The hour or two it takes to create a highly optimized Squidoo lens is well worth the effort. Build a few lenses and see what it can do for driving more traffic to your website and blog. Link building is never time wasted.

HubPages

When tackling link building for your website you have to seriously consider the highly searched HubPages. Similar to Squidoo lens, hubs are easy and quick to build as well as easily optimized. HubPages let you choose your own url, implement keywords, and even use your company name.

When building a hub avoid 'salesy' language and instead focus on supplying helpful, useful information. Hubs should have relevant hyperlinks embedded in them to your company but should bring valuable information to the reader. Add videos and images to your hubs and watch it get crawled by Google and other search engines.

Another interesting and useful aspect of HubPages is the HubScore assigned to an author. A HubScore is a grade based on a Hub owner's social media influence and the influence of their hub. Essentially, it is an indication of your content's social media value. HubScore returns valuable information in how effective you are doing in real time with social media. That HubScore is based on the amount of content and the originality of it. It is also looking for at least three outbound links on the Hub. Video is considered essential for not only attracting visitors to your page but for keeping them there as well.

Just like relevant comments on blogs help you get exposure on the web, so do your comments on other people's hubs. It builds rapport with other Hubbers but it also attracts reciprocation on your hubs. It also encourages others to backlink to your pages. Back links are critical to getting increased visibility as well as greater search engine ranking.

No matter where you decide to focus your efforts your company's website ranking in search engines depends heavily on the quality and type of back links you acquire. Using a variety of strategies that increase traffic, promote link building, and that ultimately result in an increased website conversion is the name of the SEO game.

Keeping On Track

How do you know if your site is optimized, or more importantly if your designer or developer has the skill to achieve this? A great tool is available to assist in this process and it's called Website Grader (www.websitegrader.com). While Website Grader is not the definitive answer to how good a website is, it is a great tool to compare sites and see how you, and your designer or developer stack up.

Website Grader is a free online tool that analyzes your website for the completeness of your SEO efforts. After the analysis it compares the site with their database of nearly two million sites and provides it with final score of 1 to 100. A score of 90 or better and you are doing all the right things as far as SEO is concerned. A score in the 80s shows you are working it hard and with a bit more time and effort you will be doing great. In the 70s you have some work to do but you are getting there. 50 to 70 is OK if there are no serious issues the report highlights, it may simply be you have a new site and it needs time to be searched. Less than 50 and the site is poorly done and simply is not visible to search engines (or very, very new).

What are the components of the analysis? There are a number of areas, most of which you or your designer or developer have control over, and some you don't. Here is a quick review, it is not meant to cover every item but it will give you a good idea of what is going on. Note: We have covered some of these topics earlier but we've added a bit of review here.

Meta Tags

These are your title, description and keyword fields. Using your selected keywords these fields should be completed for every page on your site. This is basic SEO, is easily performed, yet seldom done. Low hanging fruit here!

Domain Information

Search engines like to see stability from your domain name. Some sites score well because they have an old domain name, but have lousy SEO otherwise. Consider registering your domain name for two or more years at a time. That helps and is cheap.

Google Statistics

When was the last time your site was crawled by the search engines? The more often the better. Frequent crawling helps your ranking and means you have new content. Stop adding content and they come back less frequently and you slide down the charts.

Google Page Rank

Page Rank (PR) is a measure of your popularity among other sites (we discussed this earlier). While your PR as a standalone value does not matter all that much, comparing it to your competition is important. You definitely want to out rank them. As a general guide here is how you can consider PR.

0: Google doesn't think the site is very important. It doesn't get much traffic or doesn't have much useful information on it.
1-2: Google has noticed this web site and thinks it is worthy of some recognition
3-4: Google gives this web site a fair amount of authority and sees it as a decent source of information
5-6: This site is a very established source of quality information
7-8: Google says this site is a major player
9-10: These rankings are reserved for the big dogs

Alexa Traffic Rank

This is a measure of traffic starting with number one, Google and measuring up to 25 million. Of course there are far more sites than this but they stop at 25 million. Again, don't take this rating to the bank; it is a good barometer and a useful comparison. To know where your site fits in look on the chart:

1,000,000 and higher: You're basically invisible
500,000-1,000,000: On the radar

100,000-500,000: Not a major player, but worth some recognition
10,000-100,000: Getting some really good traffic, watch these sites
1,000-10,000: These guys are the professionals
< 1,000: Don't try beating them, see if you can join them

Inbound Links

Also called backlinks, inbound links are a key measure of success. In fact the entire site can be terrible SEO wise, but with enough backlinks it will rank well. Backlinks show that other sites find yours interesting. Obtaining quality backlinks is the difficult part of SEO, the processes above are easily done by most anyone after you have done the keyword research.

Getting backlinks is time consuming and involves a lot of research and in many cases using software tools or a contractor. Be cautious when using a contractor, you want your backlinks to be appropriate. If you are a building contractor you don't want your link on a Viagra site (don't laugh, you'll get offers for links like that). Normally you'll be asked to have a link to the other site on your site. As long as it's compatible then do so. If you can manage a few hundred backlinks you will have done a good job.

False Readings

There are a few warnings when reading the results of Website Grader. Well done sites that are fairly new need some time to be indexed and get some traffic. If you see the basic SEO work done right but the site is fairly new it might have a lower score. Conversely a site with relatively poor SEO work, but with a long history might be rated higher than it ought to be.

Website Grader is a great tool to check out any site and see how effective it is at SEO. Good SEO gives your site the chance it needs to be found by an Internet search. Take the time to evaluate a potential designer or developer's site. If they don't score well on their own site then imagine what they'll do for you.

An important point to remember is that generally SEO is straight forward and takes little time to implement. Effective keyword research is required ahead of time though. Building backlinks will take time, effort and likely money. However, this effort pays big dividends over time. If you take the time to work on the issues Website Grader highlights your site and your business will benefit. Know where you stand, know if your designer or developer can deliver.

Summary

All of the tasks we've discussed are only an academic and programming exercise unless you have an outcome in mind. Generally there are three outcomes; provide information, obtain leads and generate income. In all three instances your mission is well served by using the techniques I have discussed. After all you can't offer your visitor information, capture a lead or make a sale if no one comes to our site!

Like many things the web is a numbers game. Response rates generally are between 1% and 5% so in order to increase performance you need to get more visitors. Once you get a steady stream of visitors you can then work on improving response rates. After all if you want to double the number of responses you can either double the traffic or double the conversion rate! Once the traffic is in place you will find your efforts will be better spent on improving your conversion rate. However this is best left for another guide at another time!

Good luck and thanks

Web Page and Site Tune-up Checklist

The following few pages is a checklist you can use to follow along with all of the suggestions we have made earlier in the book. Fill in the blanks to keep track of where you are.

For a copy of this checklist go to:

www.practicallocalsearch.com/seobooklinks

Web Site URL:
Current Alexa Rank:
Current Page Rank (PR):
Current Web Site Grader score (of 100):

Title Tag

The title tag is displayed at the top of your browser and is the blue text at the top of every search listing. The title tag should be appropriate for each page on your site. Only your home page title tag is reviewed.

Your Current Home Page Title Tag:
Suggested Home Page Title Tag:

Description Tag

The description tag is two or three short sentences that highlight your business. This is the black text you see on a search listing and is directly under the Title (in blue). The description should be keyword and location rich and should vary with each page on your site. Only your home page description is reviewed.

Your Current Home Page Description Tag:
Suggested Home Page Description Tag:

Keyword Tags

Keyword tags are a list of your target keywords for each applicable page. These should be the words and phrases you are targeting along with geographic tags. Do not repeat yourself (on a single page). Only the home page keywords are analyzed.

Your Current Home Page Keyword Tags:
Suggested Home Page Keyword Tags:

HTML File Names

The individual pages of your site should have descriptive names. Page 1, Folder 1 and other generic page names should not be used. Page names using keywords appropriate to each page are recommended. A general overview of your page names is provided.

General Status:

Alt Tags with Images

Each image on your site should make use of an Alt tag. When a user hovers their mouse over an image the Alt tag description will show up. A few images will be reviewed and a general overview provided.

General Status:

Intra Site Links and Anchor Text

Intra site links mean you have links on individual pages to other pages on your site. Links should use effective keyword anchor text, not just "Click Here". An overall review is provided of Intra Site links and the use of anchor text.

General Status:

Accessory Pages (Contact, About, Privacy, Site Map and Links)

Each site should have these four pages. While Site Map and Privacy are seldom visited they do make the search robots happy. You should also have navigation links on all of your pages to these pages (except the Site Map which only needs a Home Page link). An overall review is provided of these pages.

General Status:

Back Links

Are other sites linking to you? If so are they appropriate to your content. An analysis of the top five sites linking to you is provided.

Top Five Linking Sites:
Are the Back Links Appropriate for Your Site:

Ease of Contact

Can your potential customers easily find out how to contact you? Surprisingly the answer is not always yes. An evaluation of all contact methods is provided (email, phone, location, map etc.).

Methods Listed:
Easy to Find on the Site:

Content Overview and Use of Header Tags

Your content should be directly applicable to your web site. There should be a few hundred words on any given page. Keywords should be used naturally throughout the content, especially in the first sentence and paragraph. H1 and maybe H2 headers should be used (one is enough normally). An overall view of how well this is being is provided.

General Status:

Your Email Address

This is not really a part of your web site however your email address is an important representation of you. Do you use a cutesy address like catfancier@emailaddress.com? Don't. This might show you are not serious or maybe people don't like cats (or whatever). Of course if your business is cat related then go for it! Do you use your ISP's email address like person@comcast.net? Don't. What if you have to change ISP providers?

I always suggest you use your name and your business domain. This is the most professional of all. Your business name and a Hotmail, Yahoo or Google Mail address are fine, but that is choice two. Please don't use AOL, many people still think of them as cheesy. Remember you can always forward a new email address to your old favorite and no one will know the difference!

Articles

Can you write articles related to your business or services? Either do so or hire a contract writer. Place the articles on your site and on a few articles directories. Find articles related to your business and post them on your site for additional content.

Blogs

If you are motivated add a blog to your site. Otherwise look for related blogs to post to using as signature block with your web site URL in anchor text.

Social Networking

Check out the major social networking sites and determine which are right for you.

Forums

Check out a few forums related to your business or expertise and see if they work for you. Be sure to use an effective signature block.

What Do I Do Next

OK, you have all of this great information. In most cases the fixes are fairly easy and quick to apply. If you have done your own web site open up your HTML or web site editor and implement the items you have highlighted in this check sheet. In other cases provide this information to your web master or designer.

Remember that maintenance of your site is an ongoing process. Don't complete this and forget about things for a year. Add content on a regular basis and the gains you make will last.

Disclaimer

This book is as accurate as possible to make it. I make no assurance any technique or suggestion described in this book will have any impact on your web site ranking or performance what so ever. In fact, no one can guarantee any alteration in the code of your web site will have any impact on its ranking in any search engine. While the techniques described in this book have been used with success by many site owners there is no guarantee you will have the same, or any success.

About the Authors

Practical Local Search
Resources for Small Business Marketing

Practical Local Search is a Seattle based company focused on developing and publishing ebooks, books, DVDs and seminars focused on small business marketing on the Internet. We strive to provide quality resources for small business owners looking to effectively compete on the web. With considerable writing, publishing, marketing and business experience small business owners will find materials and expertise to compete against local and on-line competitors.

Richard Geasey- Co Founder, Practical Local Search

Richard has a more than 20 years in the high technology industry with additional time in international trade development and small business consulting. Richard's career actually began in the military as a Captain in the Field Artillery where he learned being cold, tired and living in substandard housing was no fun. He transitioned to high technology in 1981 selling mini computers to construction companies. Moving to the high tech giant Hughes Aircraft Company he realized a big defense company was even less enjoyable than the Army.

Finally he found a home at Western Digital in Irvine CA just as the PC computer industry really started to take off.

Starting as a product manager for WD's line of Ethernet cards he ended up handling major OEMs as a marketing manager. When the Ethernet business was sold to SMC Networks he continued his work with the likes of IBM, Dell, HP and other large companies and he had the good fortune to manage International marketing for a number of years. Sadly the fun began to wind down as the hardware business turned to lower and lower margin sales. Time with Seagate Technology and tape backup drives surely highlighted that! Five years with Lantronix focusing on device marketing lead to some interesting markets like industrial automation, medical devices and other fun segments and wrapped up his hardware career. He does have a lasting legacy as the inventor of the world's only Internet BBQ.

The last few years saw time with the Australian Trade Commission as a Business Development Manager based in Seattle. In this role he worked with dozens of small Australian businesses as they created export opportunities to the US and specifically Seattle. Since then he has focused on working with small local businesses and writing books on SEO, importing, marketing on classified ad networks and local search. He also skis, bikes, hikes, plays golf and backpacks in the beautiful Northwest. Rich is the co-author of <u>Get Found Now Locals Search Secrets Exposed</u>.

Find me on LinkedIn at: <u>www.linkedin.com/in/richgeasey</u>

Email: <u>richard@practicallocalsearch.com</u>
www.practicallocalsearch.com

Shannon Evans- Co Founder, Practical Local Search

 Shannon Evans is contributing author and editor of *Your Ultimate Sales Force, Get Found Now Locals Search Secrets Exposed* and multiple businesses. Her books teach entrepreneurs that they must publish or perish in the Internet age where businesses must deliver a consistent and unified message. This is especially critical in this challenging environment of email, Internet, and mobile phones. Leveraging the market today requires new methods for attracting new clients. Shannon is recognized in the Puget Sound as an expert in how to make your business have a web presence rather than just a web page. Her conversational marketing techniques and practices will see your small business presence on the web increase.

Shannon's workshops and discussion groups are much admired by local and national professional networking groups. Whether coaching entrepreneurs on the ins and outs of writing a white paper or in how to create a website that sells, her classes are all well attended and often standing room only. Her frank, down to earth approach to Internet optimization demystifies the terms SEO and SEM for the layperson and leads the participants to a hands on session that makes them go from being one of a million to one in a million on the web.

Shannon has a wide and varied background in both the practical and the pragmatic aspects of the business world. As Co founder of Small Business Marketing Toolkits she loves nothing better than teaching local businesses how to think globally but to be searched locally. When she is not writing or teaching she can be found coaching boys' lacrosse, biking, fishing or clamming somewhere in the Seattle metro area.

Find me on LinkedIn at:

www.linkedin.com/in/pshannonevans

Email: shannon@practicallocalsearch.com

www.practicallocalsearch.com

Made in the USA
Lexington, KY
19 August 2010